JOSEF PIEPER

IN DEFENSE OF PHILOSOPHY

Classical Wisdom
Stands up to Modern Challenges

Translated by Lothar Krauth

IGNATIUS PRESS   SAN FRANCISCO

Title of the German original:
Verteidigungsrede für die Philosophie
© 1966 Kösel-Verlag GmbH & Co., Munich

Cover design by Roxanne Mei Lum
Cover border by Pamela Kennedy
Calligraphy by Joan McGrady-Beach

© 1992 Ignatius Press, San Francisco
All rights reserved
ISBN 0–89870–397–2
Library of Congress catalogue number 91–76072
Printed in the United States of America

101 PIE

IN DEFENSE OF PHILOSOPHY

CONTENTS

I

A topic by nature controversial. The first objection: Is the philosophical question answered at all? Second: the problem inherent in philosophy's subject matter: What does it mean to "encounter something"? Can we discuss the incomprehensible? Third: the sciences and reality as such. Fourth: What good is anything "not serving a purpose"? 11

II

The "philosophical" aspect. Philosophy is *not* an ordinary activity. Catharsis through the experience of death and Eros. Philosophy and praxis are incommensurable. The attempt to eliminate the discrepancy makes sense. Brentano's consoling observation. 23

III

Art and religion are philosophy's neighbors. Illusions and deceptions; religion and magic; art and "entertainment". Why "party" activists are harmless, sophists dangerous. The "interest of the day" and the "vanity of opinions" (Hegel) 33

IV

The totalitarianism of the "world of production" rejected. The meaning of "philosophy alone is free" (Aristotle). Freedom and knowledge as such. Freedom and the search for truth. In what sense is philosophy uniquely "theory"? The scientist does not keep silence but asks questions. The "gold" of philosophical silence contained in the "silver" of the scientific discourse. The "simplicity" of philosophy is more demanding than scientific "objectivity". To be "critical" in a philosophical way. "To use" and "to enjoy" (Augustine). Philosophy, meditation, loving contemplation. 41

V

What does "meaningful in itself" mean? "Good for something" in the context of personal existence. Difficulties with the arguments. What cognition achieves in the context of existence: satiated by *being*. "To see or to perish" (Teilhard de Chardin). "What do those not see . . ." Philosophical *theoria* and the *visio beatifica*. Reality as such and the nature of the spirit. Existence face-to-face with all that is. "What is this: something real?" (Aristotle). "To conceive a complete fact" (Whitehead). 57

VI

"None of the gods philosophizes" (Plato). Philosophy as "non-wisdom". Philosophy's object cannot be known. Knowledge and understanding. "The reality of a thing is also its inner light" (Thomas Aquinas). Reality as lucidity can be known. Differences with regard to Marxism. The world can be known, and yet remains unfathomable: both because it is creation. Rejection of agnostic resignation and rationalistic arrogance. 71

VII

Philosophy as "embarrassment for all" (Jaspers). "*Scientific* philosophy". A list of complaints. The infinite journey of philosophy and of existence itself. Can we achieve complete understanding? "Completeness is a phantom" (Whitehead). "Insight and wisdom seem equally dispensable." (Eliot). Science as discovery, philosophy as remembrance. The convergence of the scientific and the philosophical quest. 83

VIII

Facing the challenge. The language of philosophy and the "clarity" of expression. Misuse of language on the part of certain philosophers. Philosophy and poetry. Clarity and precision. Language and terminology. To wonder at reality as expressed in "protocol sentences". Relationship to experience. Legitimacy based on empirical roots. Leaving aside nothing. 95

IX

To include super-rational notions. Not *one* philosophy, rather philosophizing individuals. Revelation, tradition, faith, theology. The problem with a philosophy "devoid of any presupposition". Sartre's "faith". Academic sophistry is irrelevant. Can a

Christian philosopher disregard the tenets of his faith? Two voices: a believer cannot be a philosopher (Heidegger); the philosopher cannot have faith (Jaspers). Philosophy as absolute questioning, philosophy as absolute freedom: both in contrast to the traditional notion from Plato to Kant. The correlation between what is known and what is believed in philosophy defies precise description. Polyphone chords as analogy. Seeing and hearing. Conflicts to be expected. The decisive point: a conscious openness to the totality of all that is. 107

INDEX. 121

Many indispensable and important things,
such as justice,
are in themselves unprotected.
They have to be defended by those in power,
who in doing so
not only fulfill their duty
but also find their own justification.
The power of the mind, however,
for good or evil,
consists in argumentation.

I

Concerning the method used in the following reflections, I have followed to some extent the common approach employed for several centuries by the universities of medieval Christendom. As can be seen in any *articulus* of the great *Summae,* their structure would first pose, in as precise a formulation as possible, a question for discussion, together with a proposed answer, or at least with a hint of a possible answer. But then the one posing the question would keep silent for the time being, turning himself into a listener to learn the positions and objections of his opponents. More precisely, he himself, the questioner, would quote these opposing voices in the most concise and persuasive manner. Really a very demanding and difficult but also extremely convincing approach. For there would not remain any doubt that the subject matter in question could be seen from different angles, and therefore was by nature controversial—by nature: not only because the matter itself presented different objective aspects, but also because of the specific approach on the part of each searcher for knowledge, each questioning subject, who should not at all be understood as an individual, as one person, but as the many, and even more accurately, as *all* mankind. The methodology itself, therefore, brought home forcefully that the search for truth is a common human endeavor, taking place by its very nature in dialogue and discussion, also in controversy, and possibly perhaps in a controversy that could never be resolved, that would never arrive at some definitive and satisfying answer—such as would happen when dealing with a specifically philosophical topic.

Our topic—or to spell it out right away, our thesis— reads as follows: *to engage in philosophy means to reflect on the totality of things we encounter, in view of their ultimate reasons; and philosophy, thus understood, is a meaningful, even necessary endeavor, with which man, the spiritual being, cannot dispense.*

Two things are thus asserted here, and so objections might be expected to aim at these two different aspects as well. For one, this definition of philosophy proposed here could be declared wrong; or else, it could be maintained that to engage in philosophy as described here would be, if not meaningless, at least pointless.

But first we should explain more specifically what our thesis implies. At first sight, it may appear somewhat "general", perhaps even quite vague and much too innocuous. As regards "general"—well, it is supposed to be such, this is the intention. That it is not vague will become clear as we proceed. And far from being innocuous, it would be considered an act of sabotage, and rightly so, if we were to proclaim it only a few hundred kilometers to the east of here [in Communist Eastern Europe]. The meaning of our thesis all but coincides with a statement made by Alfred North Whitehead during a public symposium at Harvard University on the occasion of his seventy-fifth birthday, a statement that certainly was spontaneous but hardly unreflected, namely, that philosophy consists in the simple question,

"What is it all about?"[1] The one saying this is neither naïve nor trying to make things romantically simple; he is one of the founders of modern mathematical logic, one whose eminence as a philosopher rests not least on the fact that eventually he debunked and denounced all claims of an alleged "exact human knowledge" as self-illusion.[2] Whatever else, his description of philosophy should be seen as reflecting the realistic, unimpassioned attitude of the researcher and scientist who is allergic to all "verbal haziness".

At this point the *first* opposing voice is heard. Obviously—so the argument might go—this definition means to imply that philosophy is not really a "doctrine" dealing with a clearly circumscribed subject matter, or is it? In all other instances, when the question is: What is psychology? (What is sociology? What is physics?), the answer always begins with these words: "Psychology (or any other discipline) is the doctrine of. . . ." Yet here, are we told that engaging in philosophy would mean to ask questions, to discuss a question, or to "reflect" on something? Either the formulation is not meant to be precise, or—

Here I would interrupt my opponent, solely for his information, with this observation: No, it is not a mere tentative and unrefined formulation, as it were; on the contrary, it means exactly what it says; engaging in philosophy means indeed asking questions, reflecting on questions, and ultimately facing one single question only.

But does this question not find an answer? Does not all this questioning at least search for an answer?

[1] "Philosophy asks the simple question: what is it all about?" A. N. Whitehead, "Remarks", in *Philosophical Review* 46 (1937): 178.

[2] More about this on page 87.

Of course it does! Otherwise it would not be true questioning at all! Still, if such an answer is understood as imparting knowledge that satisfies and eliminates the question, and therefore takes away the very reason to ask the question, then we certainly have to say that philosophy's question does *not* find an answer.

If so, how then can the conclusion be avoided that philosophy and engaging in philosophy might be endeavors with scant justification, to put it mildly, endeavors that have nothing to do, at the least, with science, or even with the search for knowledge and truth?

Such an objection can obviously be raised from several angles. Those intent on empirical knowledge will, above all, talk in this manner—those who want to remain close to what is tangibly real and who reject any consideration going beyond that. But there are also those who see themselves as taking a genuinely philosophical position but affirm the same thing; I am thinking of those who propose a "scientific philosophy" and claim that the philosopher even in his proper field can and must follow the principles of the exact sciences. And then, too, the representatives of the great speculative philosophical systems of the early nineteenth century could not accept the thesis of philosophy as inquiry—neither Schelling, who calls philosophy "the science . . . of the eternal and primal forms of all things";[3] nor Hegel, who sees philosophy as "knowing the absolute";[4] nor Fichte, who states that "philosophy anticipates the totality of

[3] Friedrich Schelling, lectures on the methodology of academic studies (1802), *Studium Generale,* ed. Hermann Glockner, vol. 15 (Stuttgart: Kröner's Pocket Editions, 1954), 70.

[4] Georg Hegel, fragment of a letter to H. F. W. Hinrichs, summer 1819, *Briefe von und an Hegel,* ed. Johannes Hoffmeister, vol. 2 (Hamburg, 1953), 216.

14

all experience".[5] The high time of philosophical self-confidence, indeed, is by now entirely a thing of the past; still, it is good to remember how lofty a claim was cultivated and put forward then.

The *second* potential objection centers on something entirely different. Doubt has to be voiced, so goes the argument, regarding the subject matter with which philosophy allegedly is dealing. For one, what is the precise meaning of "the totality of things"?

As an answer I would repeat my own formulation, "the totality of things we encounter".

What does "encounter something" mean? And further, *who* encounters?

The answer to the latter question is easy: we speak, of course, about those things we, as human beings, encounter. "To encounter" something means this: within my mental horizon something turns up in such a manner as to stand in my way, as "to resist". True, in a strict sense, there cannot be anything within my horizon that would not also be in my way. I can indeed imagine something, I can produce a fantasy; but its unreal character shows precisely in its lack of resistance, its lack of standing in my way—unless I am sick. To repeat, then: I "encounter" something, means, I come upon it, I meet with it, I find it there; it stands against me as *ob-iectum,* an object. I might be able to ignore it, change it, misinterpret it for a while, maybe because of a certain simplifying "theory" or a preconceived ideology of mine. In the long run, however, such an object will assert itself, unless I simply turn away from it; it will make its presence felt, it will disturb me, make me think, "hook" me; it will be in the way.

[5] Johann Fichte, *Erste Einleitung in die Wissenschaftslehre,* ed. Fritz Medicus (Leipzig, 1944), 31.

An interjection: philosophy, therefore, would limit itself to dealing with what is encountered as *objective* reality, and not with the encountering subject?

Answer: of course, the subject as well is part of the totality encountered. I myself stand in the way of my own reflective gaze as a given and assertive reality; which means, as a reality that I, who perceive and interpret, definitely have to take into account, provided I am pursuing truth. Even should I be convinced that my *self* includes realities never to be encountered by my own perception, such distinctive traits of the subject would also be a given, something "objective", as it were, which stands in the way and cannot be ignored nor altered. And then, indeed, nothing needs to be said about the peculiar opinion that the philosopher ought to turn his attention away from all that surrounds him: "You do not reflect on anything outside, but solely on you yourself."[6] On the contrary, true philosophy deals with everything that is given, within as well as without.

All right, then, the opposing voice insists, we have this clarified; but what is the supposed meaning of the question, *"What is it all about?"* Is this not a rather imprecise formulation, more colloquial than scientific? What is this question, in essence, aiming at?

First, I would caution not to underestimate people's everyday way of speaking, neither its precision, nor its rich content, nor its importance. Many an "exegesis of common expressions" has yielded amazing results. So is anybody who in view of this or that asks, "What is it all about?", obviously presuming that the outward appearance of something, accessible to all, is not yet "all of it". Rather, there might be more to it, not readily

[6] Ibid., 6.

perceived and on the surface, some hidden source and reason, a depth not easily plumbed, a reality "behind" the mere facts. Precisely this dimension constitutes the aim of the philosopher's question. He investigates the ultimate, the "real" meaning—not of this or that but of all that is.

And this, indeed, is impossible if not altogether nonsensical, contends the opposition; on this specifically the objection is focused. Yet the request for some reasons for this finds two different answers. One answer declares the fundamental meaning of the world to be outside our perceptive powers; the other denies such fundamentals altogether.

With the first answer an appeal is made to our intellectual discipline. In Hans Reichenbach's programmatic book, *Aufstieg der wissenschaftlichen Philosophie* ["The Rise of Scientific Philosophy"], we read: "The philosopher seems incapable of controlling his craving for knowledge."[7] But is this not, we may say, an entirely appropriate observation? Our longing for knowledge is indeed beyond our control. Is this not what Plato had in mind when he compared the philosopher to a lover? The philosopher, too, is "beside himself" because he is moved to the core by the *mirandum,* the wonder of this world. We can agree wholeheartedly. What bedevils this insight, however, is the fact that Plato praises what the "scientific philosophy" rejects and disqualifies without feeling the need for further arguments: it shows a lack of discipline even to talk about things beyond our understanding!

The second answer, which accepts as real only what

[7] Hans Reichenbach, *Aufstieg der wissenschaftlichen Philosophie* (Berlin, no date [1953]), 36.

17

can be observed, expresses, of course, the unquestioned core position of every positivism. The "realism" of orthodox Marxism asserts the very same thing. Friedrich Engels called it a "philosophical whim" to speak of a hidden foundation of all reality.[8] The most direct formulation is found in the positivist manifesto, *Wissenschaftliche Weltauffassung* ["The Scientific World View"], of the early Vienna Circle: "What is, is on the surface; everything is accessible to human perception."[9] Thus it is nonsensical so much as to search for a "root" of all things or for their "ultimate reasons". In short, that mysterious object of philosophy is nonexistent. Only the objects of science are real; they are, in a strict sense and without exception, the objects of physics.[10]

This now provides the cue for a *third* objection, expressed as follows: the only possibility of perceiving the totality of all that is given consists in the collaboration among the particular sciences. This collaboration, with the purpose of shedding light on all reality, has in fact been going on for thousands of years, without the express proclamation of such a lofty intent. The individual scientist, seriously and objectively concentrating on his proper field, sees himself as just one specific component in the overall and global process of searching for knowl-

---

[8] Friedrich Engels, *Ludwig Feuerbach und der Ausgang der klassischen deutschen Philosophie* (Berlin, 1946), 17f. When the Philosophical Institute of the Academy of the Sciences in the USSR published its "Program of a Comprehensive Course in Dialectical and Historical Materialism", in 1948, it dedicated an entire paragraph to this idea, an idea also quoted by Lenin. Cf. I. M. Bochénski *Der sowjetrussische dialektische Materialismus* (Bern and Munich, 1950), 95.

[9] *Wissenschaftliche Weltauffassung. Der Wiener Kreis* (Vienna, 1929), 15.

[10] Cf. Rudolf Carnap, "Die physikalische Sprache als Universalsprache der Wissenschaft", *Erkenntnis* 2 (1931): 463, 465.

edge. Each science formulates one particular aspect; it studies only one tiny slice of reality but does so with extreme precision.

Does this not amount to confirming—so I would retort—what had been disputed in the first place: that no individual science formally poses the question that defines the identity of philosophy, namely, the question regarding the world as a totality, "What is it all about?" True, in a certain sense we may admit, with Karl Jaspers, that philosophy is "not legitimated by any object";[11] nothing, as it were, has been left over for it—unless one is willing to call the totality of all objects itself an object. This in turn depends to some extent on the kind of definitions one chooses.

And yet, this third objection does point to a real problem that is all but unsolvable. The philosopher, on the one hand, indeed does not envision some "different" reality; he looks at everything given in experience, just as does any scientist engaged in research. And even though, unlike the scientist, he ponders and questions what is given as to its ultimate reasons, he must never disregard, of course, the insights gained on the matter at hand by the appropriate sciences. Anyone who sets out, for example, to discuss the philosophical question as to the "essence" of all matter will certainly depend on the discoveries of nuclear physics. Still, on the other hand, it seems undeniable there exists a certain dimension of all reality, precisely the dimension the philosopher is concentrating on, about which the empirical sciences have little or nothing to say—so that philosophy, in this respect, remains quite independent from the sciences

[11] Karl Jaspers, *Philosophie,* 2nd ed. (Berlin, Göttingen, Heidelberg, 1948), 272.

and their eventual progress. Moreover even, the subject matter of its quest may possibly become all the more immense and unfathomable, the more the scientific exploration of the world advances. "Surrounded by the precipitous progress of the sciences",[12] so remarked Wilhelm Dilthey around the year 1900, we are nevertheless "more at a loss than in any other era" when confronted with "the one, obscure, terrifying subject matter of all philosophy".[13]

The *fourth* objection to be considered now comes from the world of practicalities and activities. No theoretical difficulties proper are voiced in it, and on a theoretical level it is not too impressive. Its importance lies in its power to define a person's life. It could be summed up as follows: philosophy, as reflection on the ultimate meaning of all that is, may indeed be possible, perhaps even quite interesting and fascinating; still, not only does it not serve any purpose, it even hampers the daily care for life's necessities. It is, therefore, nonsensical, and above all: counterproductive.

The effect of this "argument" in our contemporary world—a world ever more decisively sliding toward a situation where the notion of work reigns absolute (either dominated by the dictatorial tyranny of central planning, or by the overwhelming psychological fixation on the ideal of *efficiency*)—the effect, I believe, is so pervasive that one can all but conclude it determines the situation of contemporary philosophy much more than does philosophy's genuine quest and proper object. There certainly exist different degrees of rejection. Their span reaches, on one end, from an uncritical, unreflective

[12] Wilhelm Dilthey, *Gesammelte Schriften,* vol. 8 (Leipzig and Berlin, 1931), 197.
[13] Ibid., 140.

immersion in practicalities all the way to a deliberate setting of an absolute standard of usefulness in the most general sense, the standard of the *bonum utile,* of "bread"—a position only a small step away from the categorical indifference toward truth itself. On the one end of the scale stands the man of common active life, interested in facts, not in theory; on the other end, the wielder of power, who aggressively rejects all "useless" insights—and who, for example, would look at a philosophy not "useful" for the fostering of political action and judge it only worthy of liquidation.

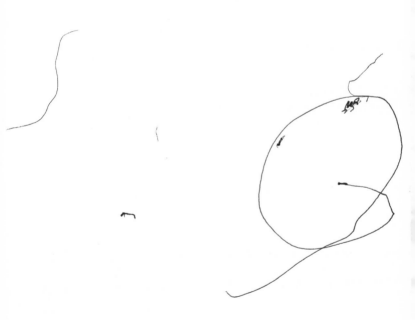

II

Those who intend to study a subject philosophically have to consider it, as the expression goes, under a certain aspect. This way of speaking and thinking rests on a notion that fails to grasp the inner nature of the philosophical endeavor. It is the notion that philosophy can be set in motion at will through a clearly defined neutral operation. Such may well be possible in a historical, or psychological, or sociological approach—and so on. In philosophy, at any rate, you do not decide to step up to a certain standpoint, and then step down again; or else, you do not turn on a special spotlight, as it were, which then would illuminate your object as to its philosophical interest. All philosophy rather flows from man's basic existential disposition toward the world, an attitude largely beyond any willful determination and decision. To approach a subject matter philosophically, to philosophize therefore—this is not a process simply at our disposal.

It follows, then, that how to philosophize is not something you can "learn"—at least not in the sense at all as you learn a foreign language, or, say, how to use a microscope: by acquiring the specific knowledge, by methodological practice, repetition, and such like. To philosophize and to "study philosophy" are two different things; one can possibly even hinder the other. Just so the poetic experience can never really be learned: neither the creative experience resulting in poetry, nor the corresponding experience by which poetry is heard or read in a poetic manner, that is, in the only meaningful manner. Henri Bremond, in his lovely book, *Mystik und Poesie* ["Mysticism and Poetry"], goes so far as to declare, "We do not really 'learn' how to swim", rather, "one day, during the first lesson, or else, after the twentieth, we suddenly realize: we are off the bottom and do not sink, we move ahead and do not walk"; indeed, we swim. "So it is with the poetic experience",[1] says Bremond. Let me add: so also it is when philosophy happens.

People are *not* commonly disposed, as they are simply not in the appropriate mood, to reflect on the ultimate meaning of reality as such. As a rule, therefore, we should obviously not expect that the philosophical experience and the philosophical quest would be such a common occurrence. "How is it with the world as such?"— this is not a question one asks while building a house, while going to court, while taking an exam. We cannot philosophize as long as our interest remains absorbed by the active pursuit of goals, when the "lens" of our soul is focused on a clearly circumscribed sector, on an objective here and now, on things that are presently "needed"—and explicitly *not* on anything else. (In intelligent company one can, of course, readily and always discuss any philosophical "problem" tossed to it from the outside like a question on a quiz show. This is not what I am talking about. Here, I understand the philosophical quest as an existential experience centered in the core of the human mind, a spontaneous, urgent, inescapable stirring of a person's innermost life.) More

[1] Henri Bremond, *Mystik und Poesie* (Freiburg, 1929), 25.

likely than not, therefore, a challenge is required that shakes the common and "normal" attitude dominating—by nature and by right—man's everyday life; a push is needed, a shock, in order to trigger the question that reaches beyond the sphere of mere material needs, the question as to the meaning of the world and of existence: to trigger the philosophical process.

A shock of this kind is the confrontation with death. For those who do not purposely ignore it, the preoccupation with the daily provisions (in the most comprehensive sense) loses its urgency instantly. Urgency, rather, is then claimed by the all-encompassing question, the philosophical question, as to the true meaning of life as such. Plato evidently knows what he is talking about when he emphasizes—often enough with unusual vehemence[2]—that familiarity with death, even a certain yearning for death, is a close neighbor of philosophy. *Factus eram ipse mihi magna quaestio,*[3] "I myself have become for me a profound question"—thus Saint Augustine concludes his report on the sudden death of a very dear friend. He who returns from such an experience (returns—to where? from where?), he who has been shaken up in such a manner, is unable to deal right away and properly with the demands of everyday life: "Leave me in peace; I am of no use right now!" Incidentally, such temporary inadequacy, unlike any sickness, is never seen as a shortcoming, not even as an inconvenience; it rather is experienced as some kind of enrichment, of liberation, of certitude that now the things of this world and of our existence are understood more deeply and evaluated more correctly than ever before.

The other existential energy linked to death, Eros,

[2] Cf. Plato *Phaedo* 64a.
[3] Augustine *Confessions* 4:4, 9.

can also affect and transform man in like manner. He who has been stirred up deeply by the power of such Eros—something of course entirely different from mere sensual arousal and desire—he, too, will unexpectedly see the world with profoundly different eyes. Again, if he does not purposely close his eyes, he too will then be confronted with the world and human existence as such. Plato should once again be remembered here; he called the mediating *daimon,* who is Eros, itself a philosophizer.[4]

At any rate, the philosopher has this in common with the one shaken up by death and the one perturbed by Eros: he as well will not fit naïvely into the functioning of the workaday routine; he as well will not be "fit" for this world; he as well will look at things differently from those who primarily are dominated by the pursuit of practical purposes. This discrepancy, this incommensurability can—so it seems—never be eliminated; it has always been with us; and there is quite some evidence that it is becoming ever more acute.

It always seemed significant to me that the history of European philosophy already in its first chapter had to report on the derisive laughter heaped upon the philosopher, and not at all without justification, by the practical everyday mind. Of course, one could easily declare the story of Thales, the stargazer who fell into the cistern, and the Thracian slave girl to be an innocuous anecdote, preserved for us purely by historical chance and proclaiming no more than a simple experience of life— one could indeed do this, were it not for the fact that Plato saw this story as expressing a serious principle. In the dialogue *Theaetetus,* Socrates tries to explain to

[4] Plato *Symposium* 204b.

26

his conversation partner, Theodorus, the almost characteristic unworldliness, as it were, of the true philosopher.[5] When this well-versed man, a mathematician,
seemingly cannot grasp anything and asks about the
meaning of all that, Socrates—speaking for Plato—answers: he means the same as is expressed in the para-
digm of Thales who was derided by a clever and witty
slave girl from Thracia for reaching out to know heavenly things while losing sight of the things right in
front of his eyes. "The very same ridicule is awaiting
everyone who engages in philosophy."[6] This is stated
with full conviction. But even so, Plato did not yet
have any idea of modern economical planning with its
total subjection to utilitarian principles. Again, the philosopher—so is declared here—remains by nature in a
state of irreconcilable discord in relation to all the clever-
ness of practical man. This is not a mere "Platonic exag-
geration" but the plain truth, as evidenced a hundred
times every day.

On my way to the university I regularly pass the
court house. And frequently I see in the front square
people engaged in lively discussion, or else, standing
together in subdued silence, obviously entirely concentrating on thoughts about *their* rights, the progress of
the trial, the chances for the defense, the sentence as it
is deemed too lenient or too strict—and so forth. Some-
times I imagine that Socrates would approach these people, whose concerns I thoroughly understand, and would
try, just as in the marketplace of Athens, to strike up
a conversation, not—and explicitly not so—concerning
who is in the right on this and who on that, but concern-

[5] Plato *Theaetetus* 173c–e.
[6] Ibid., 174a.

27

ing the very essence of justice and law, and why society cannot flourish without them. We do not have to strain our imagination much farther to see how these people would resolutely turn their backs on him, if they did not do something worse. This is an entirely natural reaction. And it is to be expected every time a philosophical question rises unexpectedly within the world of practical man (no "mediation" is possible here!)—be it the question, Why is there anything at all and not rather nothing? ("To ask this question means to philosophize", says Martin Heidegger),[7] or else, the quest to find out, in Aristotle's words,[8] what it means for something to be "real".

All the more, and with full force, does its "irrelevance" come to the fore as soon as philosophy is contrasted with the principles and hidden drives of the modern world of production. And if we call to mind that we are confronted—not by accident, after all—with new and acute challenges to our very existence, then we might easily waver somewhat in our defense of philosophy. Not only does the fight against hunger compel us to employ ever more intensive techniques for the exploitation of all available resources; the preservation of freedom as well, in this our world divided and overshadowed by competing powers, seems to demand all our energies, and rightly so. How can it be justified, then, to insist that it is essential for a truly humane existence to keep present and confront the question as to the ultimate and fundamental meaning of all that is, in short: to philosophize? On the other hand: at no time, except when there seems to be nothing left but

[7] Martin Heidegger, *Einführung in die Metaphysik* (Tübingen, 1953), 10.

[8] Aristotle *Metaphysics* 7, 1:1028b 3–4; 1003a 21.

the concern for the daily bread, at no other time will the insight that man does not live on bread alone carry such conviction. And especially when we encounter such a biblical sentence outside its familiar context and in entirely modern terms—say: as the title of a Russian novel[9] —then especially does it reveal to us its fullest and enduring meaning.

Still, it is only too understandable that every so often attempts have been made to bridge that incompatibility between philosophy and the world of production. The results have always been the same: the destruction of philosophy; for it is the weaker part. This precisely is the reason, after all, why philosophy stands in need of a defense. But then, things get rather complicated because, every now and then, the philosophers themselves attempt to eliminate this incommensurability, as they have done since time immemorial—at least since Protagoras, the Sophist, who proclaimed the purpose of pursuing wisdom, something he claims for himself, to consist in "teaching others how to deal successfully with the world".[10]

Once again, I think, it can be shown that the dynamism of such self-destruction, as it reaches our present time, turns ever more radical. We only have to compare the following three statements (whose sources shall remain unidentified for now). The first statement advocates that the place of the old theoretical philosophy should be taken by a new, practical philosophy, "which allows us to become the masters and owners of nature". The second statement declares all the achievements of human knowledge to be like tools in the great endeavor

[9] Wladimir Dudinzew, *Der Mensch lebt nicht vom Brot allein* [Man does not live by bread alone] (Hamburg, 1956).

[10] Plato *Protagoras* 318f.

of "intellectual industry". The purpose of all mental exertion would be to safeguard life and the enjoyment of life. Philosophy would set out not to understand the world but to dominate it. The third sentence declares: "Any scientist who deals with abstract problems must never forget that the scope of all science consists in satisfying the needs of society."

Anybody can see that all three statements in progressively sharper formulation express basically the same idea. The first statement goes back to Descartes;[11] the author of the second statement is the representative of American Pragmatism, John Dewey;[12] the third I have quoted, not without some malice, from the Great Soviet Encyclopedia.[13]

In the totalitarian "Workers' States" not only science but philosophy as well (or what passes for philosophy) now finds itself constantly pressured to answer the inquisitional question as to what contribution it makes to the "five-year plan". This, indeed, is nothing else but the strictest consequence of Descartes' call for a "practical philosophy". Just so is the dictator of production quotas nothing else but the contemporary embodiment of the *maître et possesseur de la nature* [master and owner of nature].

Those who try to eliminate the substantial incommensurability between philosophy and the world of production only render the philosophical endeavor inauthentic if not impossible, since the nature and dignity of this endeavor rests on its being not only outside the world

[11] René Descartes, *Discours de la Méthode,* cap. 6.

[12] Cf. G. E. Müller, *Amerikanische Philosophie,* 2nd ed. (Stuttgart, 1950), 222ff.

[13] *Bol'shaia Sovetskaia Entsiklopediia,* 2nd ed., vol. 2 (Berlin, 1952), 1317.

Above all, "the inner preoccupation with the mystery of life and of the world . . . is common to all three",[1] as Wilhelm Dilthey put it, one of the very few who, in a "Philosophy of Philosophy",[2] has devoted a steadily increasing interest, up to his later years, to the process of philosophizing as such. This interrelation and proximity manifests its power in various ways. Thus, for instance, we may from the first and without any prior knowledge presume that in any society where the genuine philosophical quest is considered "socially irrelevant", which of course can happen in many different ways and also outside of political dictatorships—we may presume, I would say, that in such a society there will not flourish the fine arts and religion either. And it is very likely, incidentally, that there will also exist a tendency as well toward trivializing death and Eros, thus depriving them of their cathartic power. And this, after all, is very true: catharsis as such does not produce efficiency.

In this era of social experiments on a grand scale, we find every now and then some confirmation, unexpected indeed, of how much the intrinsic connection between philosophy, religion, and art endures even against all odds. A ruling power may one day decide that the nation should have some poetry, simply poetry as such and nonpolitical, of course, since literature and theater dishing out nothing but party propaganda have become more and more unbearable. And so the writers and film directors are encouraged to produce, say, some comedy or a romantic story. But lo and behold, it does not work! It would succeed only if not merely this

of production, but transcendent to it, leading way beyond its confines.

Franz Brentano, Husserl's teacher and vastly influential, in his inaugural lecture in 1874 in Vienna, spoke on "The Reasons for Discouragement in the Philosophical Arena". Among the several causes for the "general distrust" he also lists "the lack of practical usefulness": "Philosophy, alone among the theoretical sciences, has not proven itself by practical results."[14] Brentano himself obviously agrees with this assessment; he sees it indeed as a serious objection. And the only counterargument he is able to offer is his hope that even for philosophy, which by nature progresses more slowly, there may eventually come "the time for an awakening to a fruitful life".[15] All the same, I do not think such encouraging consolation can convince us any more. Of greater importance, however, is the question whether we need such solace in order to avoid "distrust" or "discouragement" concerning philosophy and its genuine fruits, which nothing else can ever replace.

---

[1] Dilthey, *Gesammelte Schriften*, vol. 5, 367.
[2] Ibid., vol. 8, 204.

---

[14] Franz Brentano, *Über die Zukunft der Philosophie*, ed. Oskar Kraus (Leipzig, 1929), 92.
[15] Ibid., 99; cf. also 98.

III

Transcending the world of production occurs not
through philosophy. Other fundamental existential
deavors make it happen as well. These, too, are in pr
ple incommensurable with the world of product
and the attempt to eliminate this incompatibility
once again, only lead to the destruction of these exis
tial actions themselves. I have already mentioned *po*
which here shall stand for all the fine arts as such.
a truly great poem—a proclamation of universal pr
rigorously molded into images, forms, and soun
appears as foreign and strange in a world of useful ac
ties and practical purposes to the same extent as
the philosophical quest—this is nigh self-evident.
the more does the *religious* intention foray into an
beyond the world of practicality and gain. Not
the sentence, "Give us this day our daily bread", tho
seemingly addressing only an immediate need, not
this could be uttered as a "lifting up of the hear
God", as a prayer therefore, without at the same t
stepping beyond the confines of mere material ne
at least for one moment one would be oblivious
hunger.

Thus the philosophical, the artistic, and the religi
endeavor are indeed interconnected in a special w

well-controlled and narrow, fenced-in parcel were granted some freedom but the entire fertile landscape as well, where all those other fruits that wither under planned exploitation could equally flourish. This is thought-provoking indeed: that comedy and romantic poetry require the same fertile soil as prayer and philosophy!

And yet, more destructive and more dangerous than blatant oppression is the calculated, deceptive semblance of support. More specifically, where considerations of pure "usefulness" reign supreme, there will appear, almost inevitably, certain phony replicas, counterfeit imitations of the genuine religious, artistic, and philosophical endeavor. The danger lies in the difficulty of recognizing the deception, or rather, the self-deception; it seems, since all areas are "covered", there is nothing missing. The place of genuine prayer, for instance, may be taken by some "magical" practice, the attempt to put supernatural powers at our disposal, even to make God himself into a mere functional potency that becomes part of the utilitarian purposes of worldly calculations. Magic, so understood, is by no means something limited to primitive cults or to séances; it consistently accompanies all religious expressions as a tempting corruption. The boundary between the two is in actual fact often blurred. At what point does a prayer of petition cease to be a genuine elevation of one's self to God and therefore a liberation from the narrow confines of mere material needs? The truly religious act, without doubt, can offer possibilities of inner peace and happiness, which simply cannot be gained through any other means. Yet what is happening when religion is praised and practiced for the sake of such "success", as a means to achieve the "happy life"? After all, such an attitude is not entirely "far out"! In this, as far as I am concerned, I see the corruption and degeneration of religion into magic. And I contend that a natural affinity exists between such corruption and the exclusive pursuit of what is practical and useful.

Phony manifestations of the fine arts can also be found in various forms: say, as "entertainment" whose ultimate criterion is how "pleasing" it is (cf. Goethe: "The best works of art are utterly unconcerned with pleasing"[3]). Specifically and admittedly, with regard to the workaday operations, what happens is not transcendence but rather accommodation—which would be all right except that this threatens to make the general and limiting confinement complete and permanent.

The *littérature engagée* [activist literature] as well is a potential form of falsification, and the higher its formal quality, the more dangerous it is. Texts that in all innocence aim at "firing up the people . . . to fulfill the five-year plan"[4] or texts that declare themselves to be "weapons for socialism",[5] will not easily be mistaken by anybody for genuine poetry. Still, in the unique literary work of Berthold Brecht, for instance, where would we draw the line between poetry and propaganda?

The insidiousness of such counterfeit art, to repeat, lies in the fact that the loss is not noticed. The genuine content of religion and the fine arts is lost because people

[3] Cf. F. W. Riemer, *Mitteilungen über Goethe,* ed. Arthur Pollmer (Leipzig, 1921), 334.

[4] Address given at the Fifth Conference of the Central Committee of the Socialist Unity Party of Germany (SED). Printed in *Neues Deutschland,* March 23, 1951.

[5] Professor Kurt Hager, "Kunst ist Waffe für den Sozialismus", *Sonntag* (October 20, 1957).

delude themselves thinking it is all there. The absence of these precious gifts is not noticed because people are convinced they already fully partake of them.

Thus it is rather unlikely that a true elevation of heart and mind to God can take place in someone whose "religious" expression is formed by the manipulative attitude of inauthentic petitions—upon which he thinks himself so "pious". Likewise can it hardly be expected that in a world permeated by "light music" (or else, propagandist poetry) a genuine instance of the fine arts would yet come about at all, while everybody is nevertheless convinced of being constantly exposed to the art of music (or poetry). In the same way will any erotic catharsis become more and more improbable in an atmosphere of sophisticated or crude sexualization— for there *sex* itself is mistaken for Eros.

Pseudo-philosophy also has many faces. Rather innocuous—innocuous not in the sense as being inconsequential or without dangers, but innocuous because easily recognized—rather innocuous is the face of "practical philosophy", which stands ready to define itself as being subservient to the claims of society. When a certain German professor of philosophy declares "our philosopher comrades" to be "party activists in their specific field",[6] nobody is misled: no deception or subterfuge here. Things become more complicated when such subservience is being justified, in highly "philosophical" manner, with anthropological theories that pretend (and appear) to be sweepingly comprehensive. In this, of course, we only witness one of the countless possibilities

[6] Professor Kurt Hager, "Tagungsbericht", *Neues Deutschland* (December 17, 1957).

of "creative" thinking that has been characterized as the very domain of the Sophists.[7] Here the danger of confusion as well as self-illusion is blatantly present: "The Sophist looks exactly like a philosopher. He speaks exactly like a philosopher. In fact, it could be said he resembles a true philosopher much more than the philosopher himself."[8] In other words: it has been made extremely easy (precisely the meaning of "counterfeit"!) *not* to recognize the decisive difference.

The difference consists in this: the true philosopher, thoroughly oblivious of his own importance, and "totally discarding all pretentiousness",[9] approaches his unfathomable object unselfishly and with an open mind. The contemplation of this object, in turn, transports the subject beyond mere self-centered satisfaction and indeed releases him from the fixation on selfish needs, no matter how "intellectual" or sublime. The Sophist, in contrast, despite his emancipation from the norms of "objective" truth and the resulting claims to be "free",[10] remains nevertheless imprisoned within the narrow scope of what is "usable"—precisely because he chases after novelty, and desperately, obsessedly, tries to effect surprise by thought and expression and

[7] John Wild, *Plato's Theory of Man* (Cambridge, Mass.: Harvard University Press, 1948), 280.

[8] Ibid., 283.

[9] Johann Goethe, in a letter to Johann Herder from Rome, November 10–11, 1786.

[10] "Hence sophistry always tends to ignore the intentionality of thought, regarding reason not as the apprehension of an object, but rather as an isolated process of making hypotheses or theories in the mind. This tendency to regard reason as though it had no *object* of its own is common to modern idealism and pragmatism." Wild, *Plato's Theory*, 280, n. 36.

thus to contribute to a certain form of "higher entertainment".[11]

And so, the twofold perversion of philosophy discussed by Hegel, "On the one hand the total absorption of the mind by the interests of acute needs and the interests of the day, and on the other hand ... the vanity of personal opinions"[12] —both spring from a common root. Common to the one as well as the other, to use again Hegel's expression, is the fact that they make reason, in contradiction to its true nature, "pursue only its own interests".[13] Wherever such "selfishness" dominates the existential arena, there we should not expect true philosophy to flourish, if it can come about at all.

---

[11] Cf. Josef Pieper, "Der Verderb des Wortes und die Macht. Platons Kampf gegen die Sophistik", *Hochland* 57 (October 1964): 12–25.

[12] Georg Hegel, inaugural lecture of October 22, 1818; printed in G. W. F. Hegel, *Encyclopädie der philosophischen Wissenschaften im Grundrisse,* ed. G. Lasson, 4th ed. (Leipzig, 1930), LXXIII.

[13] Ibid.

of production, but transcendent to it, leading way beyond its confines.

Franz Brentano, Husserl's teacher and vastly influential, in his inaugural lecture in 1874 in Vienna, spoke on "The Reasons for Discouragement in the Philosophical Arena". Among the several causes for the "general distrust" he also lists "the lack of practical usefulness": "Philosophy, alone among the theoretical sciences, has not proven itself by practical results."[14] Brentano himself obviously agrees with this assessment; he sees it indeed as a serious objection. And the only counterargument he is able to offer is his hope that even for philosophy, which by nature progresses more slowly, there may eventually come "the time for an awakening to a fruitful life".[15] All the same, I do not think such encouraging consolation can convince us any more. Of greater importance, however, is the question whether we need such solace in order to avoid "distrust" or "discouragement" concerning philosophy and its genuine fruits, which nothing else can ever replace.

[14] Franz Brentano, *Über die Zukunft der Philosophie*, ed. Oskar Kraus (Leipzig, 1929), 92.
[15] Ibid., 99; cf. also 98.

III

Transcending the world of production occurs not only through philosophy. Other fundamental existential endeavors make it happen as well. These, too, are in principle incommensurable with the world of production; and the attempt to eliminate this incompatibility will, once again, only lead to the destruction of these existential actions themselves. I have already mentioned *poetry*, which here shall stand for all the fine arts as such. That a truly great poem—a proclamation of universal praise, rigorously molded into images, forms, and sounds— appears as foreign and strange in a world of useful activities and practical purposes to the same extent as does the philosophical quest—this is nigh self-evident. All the more does the *religious* intention foray into an area beyond the world of practicality and gain. Not even the sentence, "Give us this day our daily bread", though seemingly addressing only an immediate need, not even this could be uttered as a "lifting up of the heart to God", as a prayer therefore, without at the same time stepping beyond the confines of mere material needs; at least for one moment one would be oblivious to hunger.

Thus the philosophical, the artistic, and the religious endeavor are indeed interconnected in a special way.

Above all, "the inner preoccupation with the mystery of life and of the world . . . is common to all three",[1] as Wilhelm Dilthey put it, one of the very few who, in a "Philosophy of Philosophy",[2] has devoted a steadily increasing interest, up to his later years, to the process of philosophizing as such. This interrelation and proximity manifests its power in various ways. Thus, for instance, we may from the first and without any prior knowledge presume that in any society where the genuine philosophical quest is considered "socially irrelevant", which of course can happen in many different ways and also outside of political dictatorships—we may presume, I would say, that in such a society there will not flourish the fine arts and religion either. And it is very likely, incidentally, that there will also exist a tendency as well toward trivializing death and Eros, thus depriving them of their cathartic power. And this, after all, is very true: catharsis as such does not produce efficiency.

In this era of social experiments on a grand scale, we find every now and then some confirmation, unexpected indeed, of how much the intrinsic connection between philosophy, religion, and art endures even against all odds. A ruling power may one day decide that the nation should have some poetry, simply poetry as such and nonpolitical, of course, since literature and theater dishing out nothing but party propaganda have become more and more unbearable. And so the writers and film directors are encouraged to produce, say, some comedy or a romantic story. But lo and behold, it does not work! It would succeed only if not merely this

[1] Dilthey, *Gesammelte Schriften,* vol. 5, 367.
[2] Ibid., vol. 8, 204.

34

well-controlled and narrow, fenced-in parcel were granted some freedom but the entire fertile landscape as well, where all those other fruits that wither under planned exploitation could equally flourish. This is thought-provoking indeed: that comedy and romantic poetry require the same fertile soil as prayer and philosophy!

And yet, more destructive and more dangerous than blatant oppression is the calculated, deceptive semblance of support. More specifically, where considerations of pure "usefulness" reign supreme, there will appear, almost inevitably, certain phony replicas, counterfeit imitations of the genuine religious, artistic, and philosophical endeavor. The danger lies in the difficulty of recognizing the deception, or rather, the self-deception; it seems, since all areas are "covered", there is nothing missing. The place of genuine prayer, for instance, may be taken by some "magical" practice, the attempt to put supernatural powers at our disposal, even to make God himself into a mere functional potency that becomes part of the utilitarian purposes of worldly calculations. Magic, so understood, is by no means something limited to primitive cults or to séances; it consistently accompanies all religious expressions as a tempting corruption. The boundary between the two is in actual fact often blurred. At what point does a prayer of petition cease to be a genuine elevation of one's self to God and therefore a liberation from the narrow confines of mere material needs? The truly religious act, without doubt, can offer possibilities of inner peace and happiness, which simply cannot be gained through any other means. Yet what is happening when religion is praised and practiced for the sake of such "success", as a means to achieve the "happy life"? After all, such an attitude is not entirely "far out"! In this, as far as I am concerned, I see the corruption and degeneration of religion into magic. And I contend that a natural affinity exists between such corruption and the exclusive pursuit of what is practical and useful.

Phony manifestations of the fine arts can also be found in various forms: say, as "entertainment" whose ultimate criterion is how "pleasing" it is (cf. Goethe: "The best works of art are utterly unconcerned with pleasing"[3]). Specifically and admittedly, with regard to the workaday operations, what happens is not transcendence but rather accommodation—which would be all right except that this threatens to make the general and limiting confinement complete and permanent.

The *littérature engagée* [activist literature] as well is a potential form of falsification, and the higher its formal quality, the more dangerous it is. Texts that in all innocence aim at "firing up the people . . . to fulfill the five-year plan"[4] or texts that declare themselves to be "weapons for socialism",[5] will not easily be mistaken by anybody for genuine poetry. Still, in the unique literary work of Berthold Brecht, for instance, where would we draw the line between poetry and propaganda?

The insidiousness of such counterfeit art, to repeat, lies in the fact that the loss is not noticed. The genuine content of religion and the fine arts is lost because people

[3] Cf. F. W. Riemer, *Mitteilungen über Goethe,* ed. Arthur Pollmer (Leipzig, 1921), 334.

[4] Address given at the Fifth Conference of the Central Committee of the Socialist Unity Party of Germany (SED). Printed in *Neues Deutschland,* March 23, 1951.

[5] Professor Kurt Hager, "Kunst ist Waffe für den Sozialismus", *Sonntag* (October 20, 1957).

delude themselves thinking it is all there. The absence of these precious gifts is not noticed because people are convinced they already fully partake of them.

Thus it is rather unlikely that a true elevation of heart and mind to God can take place in someone whose "religious" expression is formed by the manipulative attitude of inauthentic petitions—upon which he thinks himself so "pious". Likewise can it hardly be expected that in a world permeated by "light music" (or else, propagandist poetry) a genuine instance of the fine arts would yet come about at all, while everybody is nevertheless convinced of being constantly exposed to the art of music (or poetry). In the same way will any erotic catharsis become more and more improbable in an atmosphere of sophisticated or crude sexualization— for there *sex* itself is mistaken for Eros.

Pseudo-philosophy also has many faces. Rather innocuous—innocuous not in the sense as being inconsequential or without dangers, but innocuous because easily recognized—rather innocuous is the face of "practical philosophy", which stands ready to define itself as being subservient to the claims of society. When a certain German professor of philosophy declares "our philosopher comrades" to be "party activists in their specific field",[6] nobody is misled: no deception or subterfuge here. Things become more complicated when such subservience is being justified, in highly "philosophical" manner, with anthropological theories that pretend (and appear) to be sweepingly comprehensive. In this, of course, we only witness one of the countless possibilities

[6] Professor Kurt Hager, "Tagungsbericht", *Neues Deutschland* (December 17, 1957).

of "creative" thinking that has been characterized as the very domain of the Sophists.[7] Here the danger of confusion as well as self-illusion is blatantly present: "The Sophist looks exactly like a philosopher. He speaks exactly like a philosopher. In fact, it could be said he resembles a true philosopher much more than the philosopher himself."[8] In other words: it has been made extremely easy (precisely the meaning of "counterfeit"!) *not* to recognize the decisive difference.

The difference consists in this: the true philosopher, thoroughly oblivious of his own importance, and "totally discarding all pretentiousness",[9] approaches his unfathomable object unselfishly and with an open mind. The contemplation of this object, in turn, transports the subject beyond mere self-centered satisfaction and indeed releases him from the fixation on selfish needs, no matter how "intellectual" or sublime. The Sophist, in contrast, despite his emancipation from the norms of "objective" truth and the resulting claims to be "free",[10] remains nevertheless imprisoned within the narrow scope of what is "usable"—precisely because he chases after novelty, and desperately, obsessedly, tries to effect surprise by thought and expression and

[7] John Wild, *Plato's Theory of Man* (Cambridge, Mass.: Harvard University Press, 1948), 280.

[8] Ibid., 283.

[9] Johann Goethe, in a letter to Johann Herder from Rome, November 10–11, 1786.

[10] "Hence sophistry always tends to ignore the intentionality of thought, regarding reason not as the apprehension of an object, but rather as an isolated process of making hypotheses or theories in the mind. This tendency to regard reason as though it had no *object* of its own is common to modern idealism and pragmatism." Wild, *Plato's Theory,* 280, n. 36.

thus to contribute to a certain form of "higher entertainment".[11]

And so, the twofold perversion of philosophy discussed by Hegel, "On the one hand the total absorption of the mind by the interests of acute needs and the interests of the day, and on the other hand . . . the vanity of personal opinions"[12] —both spring from a common root. Common to the one as well as the other, to use again Hegel's expression, is the fact that they make reason, in contradiction to its true nature, "pursue only its own interests".[13] Wherever such "selfishness" dominates the existential arena, there we should not expect true philosophy to flourish, if it can come about at all.

---

[11] Cf. Josef Pieper, "Der Verderb des Wortes und die Macht. Platons Kampf gegen die Sophistik", *Hochland* 57 (October 1964): 12–25.

[12] Georg Hegel, inaugural lecture of October 22, 1818; printed in G. W. F. Hegel, *Encyclopädie der philosophischen Wissenschaften im Grundrisse,* ed. G. Lasson, 4th ed. (Leipzig, 1930), LXXIII.

[13] Ibid.

IV

Whoever intends to refute the objection that philosophy does not serve any purpose and therefore is a nonsensical endeavor without any justification—whoever sets out to show, in contrast, why it is yet beneficial to philosophize—has to begin his answer by accepting the objection, at least its first part, by explicitly agreeing with it, by even confirming it, and by understanding it perhaps much more categorically than the opponent himself. Indeed, it is true: philosophy does not serve any purpose—not only as a matter of fact, but because it cannot and must not serve any purpose! In the words of Martin Heidegger: "It is entirely proper and perfectly as it should be: philosophy is of no use."[1]

The aggressive tone that emerges here derives not only from the wording but from the thought itself. By declaring that reflection on reality as such—that is, philosophy—is a meaningful, even necessary human endeavor, while admitting its lack of practical usefulness, I have in fact already rejected the totalitarian claim of a commercialized world. With this I have already denied that some five-year plan could ever be held up as the decisive standard. I have affirmed that there is an existential realm in which such categories as "profit",

[1] Heidegger, *Einführung in die Metaphysik*, 9.

"feasibility", "usefulness", "efficiency" mean nothing, a realm that nevertheless is indispensable for a truly human existence.

What appeared, at first sight, as an embarrassment, a defect, a shortcoming reluctantly admitted—does this now turn out to be, on the contrary, a distinction, even a privilege rightfully claimed and affirmed?

Indeed, it does! This privilege is called "freedom". Philosophy by its nature is a free endeavor, and for this reason it serves no one and nothing!

At this point we should certainly consider one very distinct dimension of the concept of "freedom". This dimension was always implied in the traditional Western concept of freedom, and yet a clear understanding of it is not easy to come by. First of all, we have to eliminate the misconception of freedom as nothing more than political and civil liberties. These, of course, are included and cannot possibly be ignored, but they are not what "freedom" here means. This is one of the reasons why any discussion of this issue with politicians and sociologists usually ends in discord. Noninterference by outside powers such as the government is not the primary meaning of this specific freedom; we envision rather a certain inner quality. We speak of "freedom" in the same sense as is implied in a concept from antiquity, the ancient notion of the *artes liberales,* the "liberal arts". "Academic freedom" should also be mentioned here; this, too, originally meant something different from a mere instance of political freedom of speech, or the students' privilege of pursuing their studies at their own discretion.

Aristotle seems to be the first to have formulated explicitly the precise nature of this kind of freedom. He deals with it in a dense, not easily deciphered section of his *Metaphysics*, in direct connection with philosophy.[2] Indeed, philosophy *alone* would be free in this specific sense. In what sense, then? Analyzing Aristotle's text in his *Metaphysics*, we find to our amazement that "free" there means the same as "nonpractical"! "Practical" is everything that *serves* a purpose. Precisely this, then, does not apply to philosophical reasoning or *theoria*. Philosophy is "free" insofar as it is not geared toward some purpose outside itself. Philosophy, rather, is an endeavor containing its own meaning and requires no justification from a purpose "served".

I suspect that this, at first sight, does not sound very convincing. Above all, is this not an assertion rather than an argument? And besides, are we not playing here a bit with tautology?

Quite a few things, indeed, come into play here. Our topic is not far, as it were, from the hub of the wheel where all the spokes just about touch each other. And after all, in this area we can hardly expect any proof presented *more geometrico* [with mathematical stringency]. On closer scrutiny, it seems to me, there are three distinct thoughts tied together in Aristotle's statement. The first thought concerns the connection between knowledge and freedom; the second touches on the uniqueness of the philosophical *theoria* [reasoning], while the third, being the most relevant here, tries to answer the question as to the reason why philosophy is an endeavor meaningful in itself. We do well briefly to discuss these points in proper order.

With regard to the *first* point I wish to relate an experience of several years ago that brought home to me, suddenly and quite forcefully, some important insights.

[2] Aristotle *Metaphysics* I, 2:982b 27.

In those days it still was possible, though only halfway legal, for groups of students from the [East German] totalitarian area to visit us [in West Germany] for talks and discussions. In one such circle there was mentioned, casually, a novel that at that time enjoyed much public attention but by now is virtually forgotten. When asked, our friends from "over there" reported that this novel would not be published in their country because it contained serious historical errors about the Russian Revolution, which in reality (for example) had by no means stifled the development of the individual. We replied that such things, after all, could be researched and determined objectively—could they not? For this, of course, a totally independent discussion would be required, not necessarily a discussion in public but at any rate without "official" interference. It was further pointed out that there had to be, after all, some free space in society where such discussion could take place unimpeded. The conversation, which had begun innocently enough, at this point suddenly brought home something quite decisive—to all participants, not only to those from "over there". More precisely, two things became strikingly evident.

First, how important it is whether or not such a "free" space exists in a political commonwealth, a space where in fact and contrary to the proclaimed maxim[3] "the class struggle is suspended", as well as the five-year plan, and all "politics" to boot, all special interests, be they collective or private. A space of precisely this kind is meant by the ancient term *scholē,* which designates "school" and "leisure" at the same time. It means a

[3] Professor Dr. Scheler at a meeting on contemporary tasks of philosophy; reported in *Neues Deutschland* (December 17, 1957).

refuge where discussion takes place, in total independence—that is, without the interference of practical goals—on just one question: How are things, "What are the facts?"

And this, secondly, suddenly sprang fresh into focus: this free space, true, must be safeguarded and protected from without by political power, but the possibility, even the very constitution of its freedom derives primarily from within—from nothing else than the irrepressible determination to search for the truth, the exclusive interest, be it only for this specific moment, to find the true facts about the matter in question.

No one would find it difficult nowadays to imagine a world whose environment is almost entirely determined by a public parlance consisting of mere "slogans". All pronouncements would be made "in order to . . ." and "for the purpose of . . ."; they say nothing, they rather intend to effect something. Yet with all this, would something else not be quite evident as well: whoever could manage to keep a keen eye on the truth of things, though surrounded by the obstruction of proclamations, banners, and slogans; whoever could manage to declare from the heart what is true and real, be it only silently and to himself (such as, "But the emperor has no clothes")—such a person would have preserved for himself a truly free space!

Once again we need to recall the original meaning of a common and seemingly familiar term. *Theoria* and "theoretical" are words that, in the understanding of the ancients, mean precisely this: a relationship to the world, an orientation toward reality characterized entirely by the desire that this same reality may reveal itself in its true being. This, and nothing else, is the meaning of truth; nothing else but the self-revelation

45

of reality. Thus we may state that the contemplation of reality is properly called "theoretical" whenever the aim is to discover the truth and nothing else. With this I have once again quoted, almost verbatim, Aristotle's *Metaphysics*.[4]

Never and nowhere else, except in the living and actual *theoria* of philosophy, is there found such a radical independence with regard to every imaginable subordination under practical goals. This very independence is meant when we speak of the "freedom" of philosophy.

Truth and knowledge on one side, freedom on the other, are thus interrelated in a quite specific, definite sense. Perhaps it no longer sounds so strange when the medieval definition calls "liberal arts", *artes liberales*, "only those that are oriented toward knowledge alone".[5] In the same way, and bearing in mind such experiences and reflections, the old line about the "truth that sets us free" (Jn 8:32) shows, suddenly and unexpectedly, a rather young, original, and also serious face.

But now, the second question: Why, in all the world, should the "theoretical" dimension be the *defining* characteristic of philosophy? Does not every science equally pursue just this, to see all things as they really are? And do we not, therefore, find *theoria* here also, together with the freedom that goes with it? The answer, as is to be expected, cannot be expressed in simple and one-dimensional terms.

Theoria, as existential human act, aims—as we have stated—at the unqualified cognition of reality, at truth

---

[4] Aristotle *Metaphysics* 2, 1:993b 20.

[5] "Illae solae artes liberales dicuntur, quae ad sciendum ordinantur." Thomas Aquinas, *In duodecim libros metaphysicorum expositio* 1, 3; no. 59.

and nothing else. The potency to know reality is indeed none but reason itself; even our capacity of speech indicates as much. The nature of reason, then, manifests itself most genuinely in the very act of *theoria;* in this alone is reason completely actuated. But then: *to perceive means to listen in silence.* "Though it has been said many times before, it will not hurt to say it once again":[6] the invisible alone is transparent, and only in silence is hearing possible. Moreover, the stronger the determination prevails to hear all there is, the more profound and more complete the silence must be. Consequently, philosophy (as contemplation of reality as such and as the highest possible actualization of *theoria*) means: to listen so perfectly and intensely that such receptive silence is not disturbed and interrupted by anything, not even by a question.

This precisely constitutes the difference between the individual sciences and philosophy. Science does not remain silent; it asks questions. It is the very nature of its questions that establishes a particular branch of science. Francis Bacon even compared the method of experiments employed by science to a "painful interrogation", an expression meaning "torture", through which nature would be forced to yield an answer.[7] This, of course, is an extreme yet not entirely inappropriate comparison. Not at all do I mean to imply that it would be improper and illicit to subject nature to such a "tortured" interrogation. And it is indeed possible, even necessary, for the acquisition of true knowledge about reality at all that answers thus elicited be absorbed in listening silence, that is, with the attitude

[6] Plato *Georgias* 508d.
[7] Francis Bacon, *De dignitate et augmentis scientiarum* 2, 2.

of *theoria*. Except that, in the case of science, this silence is not perfect; it is interrupted and limited by the explicit formulation of a specific and particular aspect under which the object, "the world"—in itself infinitely complex—shall be questioned. It pertains to the nature of such a formulated question that the direction of the answer is already determined. In other words: entire realms of reality are expressly "of no interest" right from the start. Seen from this angle, the philosopher's question, strictly, is no question at all: *What is it all about?* It rather articulates, as it were, the very attitude of silence, a silence that in total and undistracted openness extends into the world, listening. In this respect, the objection on the part of the exact sciences, that there is altogether not even the possibility to express such a question, is right on target. Whoever reflects on the world "under every conceivable aspect" (we leave undecided what a "conceivable" aspect might be!) obviously does not consider it "under a particular aspect"! Nevertheless, this is precisely the manner in which philosophy approaches its object, this object being reality and existence as such.

The scientific approach to reality, by resolutely defining and exploring a specific aspect, indeed does not assume an attitude of complete and receptive silence. Of course, with all this we do not in the least mean to say that such an approach is not justified; this would be absurd. On the contrary and clearly, the scientific approach is even absolutely indispensable for our life. On this, there should not be the slightest misunderstanding.[8] And, incidentally, within the domain of

[8] See for instance Otto Seel, *Die platonische Akademie* (Stuttgart, 1953), 45ff. Cf. Josef Pieper, *Was heisst Akademisch?,* 2nd ed. (Munich, 1964), 126.

scientific research, which certainly is not only something abstract ("science as such") but is pursued by living human beings, often enough some furtive philosophizing takes place. This concealed dimension, more
sensed than seen, seems to me to be after all the true
"academic" content of any science. It means that the
silver of scientific discourse is mingled with the golden
silence of philosophy.[9]

It should be obvious that such "silence" has nothing
to do with any neutral and passive posture, much less
does it flow from it. It is rather sustained by a commit-
ment anchored in the soul's innermost core, really by
the interest and the concern not to miss any dimension
of the totality of all that is real. At the same time,
there is, of course, no doubt at all that this totality
will never be perfectly understood; yet all the same,
nothing of it must ever be deliberately excluded, covered
up, forgotten, or suppressed. This openness for the
whole is truly some kind of distinctive badge; it defines,
as *differentia specifica* [specific difference], all true philosophy.

Concerning this openness we should further add that
it presupposes (if it is not identical with) a total and
unbiased candor reaching much deeper into man's existential core than the realism we call "scientific objectivity". The search for a better technical procedure, or
research into the causes of certain diseases—such tasks,
even should they occupy my mind day and night, do
not engage a person's existential core. In order to be
able to answer such questions pertinently and adequately, apart from the necessary scientific qualifica-
tions, it is quite inconsequential what kind of person I

[9] Cf. Pieper, ibid., 22ff.

49

am. For such a task the unbiased candor of the philosophical approach is not demanded. Its absence will not prevent me from being highly successful in scientific research; it will, however, undoubtedly prevent any true philosophy, that is, my reflecting with unbiased sensitivity—say, on the ultimate significance of man's mortality. In this, mental acuteness will not achieve very much, no matter how much intelligence is involved. What is demanded here is a total and serene unfolding of the most intimate responsive powers of the soul, a process that does not yield to man's disposing will. It seems that the traditional wisdom of the Far East has preserved this awareness much more vividly than our Western *ratio* [rationality].

We could characterize this personal precondition for all true philosophy with Goethe's powerful formulation, already mentioned earlier: "a total shedding of all pretensions".[10] Even more to the point is the way the Bible speaks of the "guileless eye" (*simplicitas*) that gives light to the whole body.[11] Only a simplicity of this kind, which cannot coexist with any prejudice, enables us to behold at all the ramifications of philosophy's genuine object.

One might perhaps object here that nobody could ever fully satisfy such a demand. Indeed! All the same, the very practical and consequential significance of that demand is revealed by what it formally excludes and denies.

At this point we should emphasize that not only is science *not* in the same radical sense *theoria* as is philoso-

[10] Goethe, letter to Herder.

[11] Mt 6:22. In Luther's translation: "Wenn dein Auge einfältig ist, so wird dein ganzer Leib licht sein; ist aber dein Auge ein Schalk, so wird dein ganzer Leib finster sein."

phy, but it moreover stands in a specifically different relation to freedom. There may even be a particular form of mental constraint that afflicts only those who reason scientifically, precisely when they venture into philosophy—or to put it more cautiously—when they try, in their own ways, to determine what the world as such is all about. Whoever then claims to use the approach undoubtedly appropriate for science by saying, for instance: I disregard, now as philosopher, anything that cannot be demonstrated cogently and proved critically, I am interested only in things "clear and distinct"— such a one would already have distorted the genesis of the philosophical quest. He already would have excluded the mental openness that is the mark of the philosopher *per definitionem,* the openness for the unabridged object of human cognition, that is: for reality as such, to be contemplated under any conceivable aspect. What makes him so sure that there are no possible insights into reality, which are in fact true and yet can neither be verified nor defined "clearly and distinctly"? (Incidentally, nobody could stay alive even one day unless he accepted as true numerous insights of precisely such kind.) How do we know that it may not be in fact those realities "most obvious in themselves" to which our mind relates like the eyes of nocturnal birds to the light of day[12] — as Aristotle asserts? A "critical attitude", for the philosopher, does not primarily mean accepting only what is absolutely certain, but being careful not to suppress anything.[13]

Another characteristic of the correlation between science and freedom consists in the fact that science, because

[12] Aristotle *Metaphysics* 2, 1:993b 9.
[13] Cf. Josef Pieper, *Über den Glauben* (Munich, 1962), 81f.

of its practical outlook, can be employed for utilitarian goals—which is entirely proper, that is, it does not in any way diminish the dignity of science. Nobody has ever complained about medical science being employed for the practical purpose of treating illnesses, or about chemistry and physics being used to solve technical problems. This practical aspect, however, inevitably contains the potential for both use and abuse. It is well known that some of the first atomic scientists have tried to prevent the technical exploitation of their discoveries. This is simply impossible, as impossible as to prevent, say, the exploitation of psychoanalytical discoveries for promoting business; all this lies in the nature of such things!

There is no need at all to object to the famous Marxist demand to "transform the world". On the contrary, it is good and even necessary to transform the world, not only nature but the human condition as well. Yet it becomes evident, already at this point, that it is no less good and necessary to know the world and to "interpret" it, in a purely theoretical manner, which means being guided by the desire for truth and nothing else. It is moreover quite impossible and hopeless to transform the world in any meaningful way without having first perceived what the world is basically all about. That specific dimension of the world, of course, which absorbs the philosopher's interest, remains in principle outside any conceivable scheme to transform the world, remains beyond all utilization and exploitation.

Saint Augustine has emphasized the distinction between *uti* = to use, and *frui* = to enjoy, and especially between those things that we use and other things that we enjoy yet cannot and must not use.[14] To enjoy a

---

[14] Augustine *De doctrina christiana* 1, 3f.; *De Trinitate* 10, 10.

thing means: to accept it for and by itself and to find joy in it. To use a thing, on the other hand, says: "to make something the means to obtain what we enjoy".[15] Perhaps we could say that philosophical contemplation is concerned with those things "that we enjoy". But this way of putting it can easily be misunderstood. It becomes clearer only if we add one other thought.

The Romans translated the Greek word *theoria* with the Latin word *contemplatio*. In the Latin translations of Aristotle's main work as well, the *Metaphysics*, used by Thomas Aquinas for his commentary, we read: *theoria id est contemplatio*.[16] As soon as the concept of "contemplation" appears in this context, there has come to the fore—unexpectedly—another aspect that so far has been hidden but now can be identified. It was doubtless part of the ancient Platonic-Aristotelian conception of *theoria* and now completes as well our own idea of what it means, and what it might imply, to philosophize. The philosophical *theoria*, at least in its fullest expression, may in its actual occurrence indeed be almost indistinguishable from "contemplation" as conceived by the later era, the Christian West.

Now, however, "contemplation" means a *loving* gaze, the beholding of the beloved.[17] We have to raise the question, then, whether philosophical reflection on reality as such may not equally presume or imply some kind of acceptance of this same reality. I hesitate to use the word "love", because it is too big. "Acceptance", on the other hand, seems too imprecise and too weak. Even those who are simply incapable of any philosophical *theoria* because they consider the objects of the world,

[15] Cf. Thomas Aquinas, *Scripta super libros Sententiarum* 1d 1.

[16] Aristotle *Metaphysics* 2, 1:993a 30.

[17] Cf. Josef Pieper, *Glück und Kontemplation*, 3rd ed. (Munich, 1962), 74.

and perhaps even human beings (excepting themselves), as so much raw material that may be useful for some purpose—even those "masters and owners of nature" could be said in a certain sense to accept reality and find it good: good, of course, for them and their aims. For the true philosopher, however, the challenge seems to be this: to acknowledge, before any consideration of specifics and without regard to usefulness, that reality *is good in itself*—all things, the world, "being" as such; yes, all that exists, and existence itself. Do we not call "desire" (*amor concupiscentiae*) our accepting attitude toward those things that are "good for us and our purposes"? And does not the acceptance of that alone which we deem "good in itself" properly deserve the name of "love"? If we consider now the precise meaning of that ancient and for us moderns somewhat enigmatic expression, "All that is, is good", *omne ens est bonum,* we find that it does not say anything substantial if not this: the world, as creation, is willed by God, which means that it is created *in love* and is therefore, by its very existence, good. That we use the term "love" here is, of course, not decisive (even though, on the other hand, we should not call a primordial reality simply a "term"). What is decisive, though, is our intention to identify a precondition, not readily evident, of all philosophical *theoria*. This qualification may be more successful, indeed, if we use a negative formulation and put the following question before us: Is not philosophy, as human endeavor, equally threatened by the totalitarian demands of the marketplace *and* by the nihilistic dogma that the world as such is absurd, that any kind of being deserves to perish?[18] And should the possibility not be

[18] Cf. F. Nietzsche, *Wille zur Macht* (1980), 24.

recognized that both these threats may be linked by some hidden connection?

And we are still in the business of interpreting those unbelievably concise ten lines of Aristotle's *Metaphysics*! Their meaning must indeed remain inaccessible to anybody who does not recognize and accept their hidden implications. Two of them have been discussed so far: the—literally—liberating power of the desire for truth; and the conviction that this desire for truth is most completely fulfilled in the philosophical *theoria*. The insights gained, so far, we hope, are twofold: not only that "knowledge is eminently 'free' whenever it is philosophical knowledge",[19] but also that science is indeed dealing with the truth, and yet, that it is philosophy alone that in the strictest sense represents, in Aristotle's own words, "the science of truth",[20] *maxime scientia veritatis.*[21]

[19] J. H. Newman, *The Idea of a University*, 5, 5.

[20] Aristotle *Metaphysics* 2, 1:993b 19f.

[21] Aquinas, *In duodecim libros* 2, 1; no. 297. "Si ergo huic conjunxerimus, quod . . . philosophia prima non est practica, sed speculativa, sequetur quod recte debeat dici scientia veritatis." Ibid., no. 290. ". . . Quod philosophia prima *maxime* consideret veritatem." Ibid., no. 291.

V

And yet, in the end, all this reasoning becomes again doubtful unless it is possible to answer this question (*our third point*): such purposeless and "free" reflection on reality as such, exclusively aiming at truth and thus entirely "theoretical"—what makes this an endeavor *meaningful in itself?*

How are we to understand this characterization "meaningful in itself"? I am not so sure a certain possible misunderstanding is in fact lurking here; I shall mention it anyway. "Meaningful in itself" does, of course, not say: meaningful *apart from the human person,* as if we were talking here about, say, conformity to some abstract and independently "valid" norms. Rather, the point of reference is most clearly the human existence. "Meaningful in itself" are those realities that in a specific sense stand in reference to the human person and to human existence.

This, however, does not at all amount to making man an absolute. It does imply, though, that man, in a certain sense, is also "meaningful in himself". The very same thought, for instance, is expressed by the complicated concept of "person". A being existing for the purpose of its own perfection: thus, in a simplified (yet not altogether illicit) formulation, could we define the meaning of "person". Such a definition, of course, applies only to the individual. The individual alone, in this sense, is in truth an entity and someone; and he alone, strictly speaking, is to be respected for what and who he is, and not to be used as a means for any purposes outside his own self.[1] With this we have indeed proclaimed something rather consequential, something that has consequences also regarding the dignity (and the import) of the philosophical act, which cannot be conceived except as emanating from the human person. It is true, wherever the decisive origin of human accomplishments is declared to be "society" (or, say, the "Universal Spirit", or "matter", or "the Cosmos", or "evolution"), there is also declared, *eo ipso,* that the individual person neither represents nor achieves anything meaningful in itself, be this achievement philosophy or whatever else.

As an initial approximation we may state, therefore, that "meaningful in itself" means "being good for something within the context of personalized human existence". "Being good for something"—this expression, in a preliminary way already employed earlier in contrast to "useful for", needs a more precise definition, as has become evident by now. Bread, too, is "good for something", namely, to still and satisfy hunger. To still one's hunger, in turn, is good for staying alive and not falling ill. To be healthy, to exist bodily—what, then, is such good for? Is this a legitimate question at all? Evidently, we are approaching here a certain limit. Still, we could answer: it is good for being truly human; for "becoming

---

[1] Thomas Aquinas asserts that even divine providence would govern the human person "for the man's own sake", taking literally the striking biblical expression (Wis 12:18) that has God guiding us "with great reverence", *cum magna reverentia. Summa contra gentiles* 3, 112.

what you are"; for doing what is good; for "glorifying God"—and so on. But at this point we have reached the end of the line, when it becomes pointless to ask further questions ("What good is it to live a meaningful human life?"). At this point, we do not discuss any longer what something is "good *for*" but we talk about *the Good* as such, about the *bonum hominis*[2] itself [man's good] and everything implied in this concept.

The same context is also evoked by the earliest utterance coming down to us from the city of Athens, predating Plato by one hundred years. It is Anaxagoras' answer to the question posed to him, "Why are you here on earth?" His reply: to behold in contemplation, *eis theorian,* the sky and the order of the universe.[3] This is the very same notion advanced by our thesis here: that the philosophical reflection on reality as such is a human endeavor meaningful in itself; that is it not merely "oriented toward" or contributing to "man's good", but constitutes an essential element of such good itself—including, to be sure, also the common good, the *bonum commune.* The good of man's common life requires the philosophical *theoria,* the contemplation directed toward truth alone (which, of course, can be undertaken by none but the individual, the person), and this, again, not so much as a "service" to the commonweal, as a "contribution" to it, but rather as an indispensable constituent of the common good itself.[4]

[2] Thomas Aquinas, *Quaestiones disputatae de virtutibus in communi* 9.

[3] Cf. Aristotle *Eudemian Ethics* I, 5:1216a 15. Clement of Alexandria *Stromata* 2, 130, 2. Diogenes Laertius, *Lives of Eminent Philosophers* 2, 3; no. 10.

[4] Cf. Aquinas, *Sententiarum* 4d 26, 1, 2.

Very well, then; with this, our thesis has become somewhat clearer. And yet, it still remains nothing more than an assertion. The question is: How about some pertinent arguments? There we face a dilemma. Our thesis, and any pertinent argumentation as well, does not merely talk *about* philosophy but itself qualifies as philosophy. To reflect on it already means to philosophize—and thus to be subject to the preconditions of that specific openness and simplicity I have mentioned earlier. This does not imply the utter absence of any solid argument bearing on an "objective" evaluation; it does imply, though, that any argumentation would boldly presume the willingness to converse on a level much deeper than the mere rational surface.

Our arguments here will propose two considerations: first, the import and the function of theoretical cognition within the framework of human existence; and secondly, the very specific correlation tying the object of the philosophical *theoria* to the very nature of the human spirit.

First: What, in essence, occurs when man comes to know reality, when he sees a thing as it really is? In the Western philosophical tradition, this question finds an unexpectedly unanimous answer. What occurs, so we hear, is an appropriation of reality in a manner so intensive as having no parallel anywhere else, a conquest of what is, *conquête de l'être,*[5] a taking possession, an assimilation, an incorporation—literally a feeding and filling on *being.* Plato, in his vision of the Great Banquet in the "heavenly beyond", describes the soul as beholding, in utter bliss, the essence of Being-in-Truth, and thus receiving its nourishment.[6] This is not meant as a

[5] Pierre Rousselot, *L'intellectualisme de Saint Thomas* (Paris, 1936) XVI.

[6] Plato *Phaedrus* 247d 3–4.

mere allegorical image, no more than Saint Thomas' word of knowledge as the most noble way of owning something, *nobilissimus modus habendi aliquid*.[7]

Such manner of speaking, incidentally, is not so foreign to what is familiar to us as may seem at first. We are in fact well aware and do not need a special reminder, for example, that we do not really make anything "our own" by mere acquisition or juridical procedure, anything we in truth call "ours" and "mine". Rather, anything we wish or imagine to possess (a garden, a book, a painting; but also a friend, a teacher, a lover; yes, even unrepeatable events or encounters)—all this is "part of us" only to the extent that we keep it in our presence: by beholding it ever anew, by contemplation, reflection, and recollection. By no other means will we ever own our true wealth, our personal and living possession. To be convinced of this we hardly need the confirmation through the "wisdom of the ancients".

To find such affirmation we do not even have to invoke only the ancient sages. Pierre Teilhard de Chardin prefaced his book *The Phenomenon of Man* with a surprising and at first seemingly misplaced prologue, entitled, "To See".[8] There we read that the ability to see, in a certain sense, encompasses "the very essence of life"; that "the sharpness and scope of the beholding gaze is the measure of perfection"; that indeed the principle of all progress in the evolution of life could be compressed into the formula, "the fashioning of ever more perfect eyes", *élaboration d'yeux toujours plus parfaits*. "To see or to perish": this would be, in all dimensions of the universe, "the challenging situation im-

[7] Thomas Aquinas, Commentary on the *Liber de causis* 18; cf. also Aquinas, *Sententiarum* 4d 49, 3, 5, 1 ad 2.
[8] Pierre Teilhard de Chardin, *Le phénomène humain* (Paris, 1955).

posed on us by the mysterious gift of our existence".[9]

Teilhard's formulation of this frightening alternative, *voir ou périr,* implies one other challenge that is easily overlooked. It proposes the thought that perhaps the counterpart most perfectly opposed to "perdition" might be defined as the most perfect ability to "see"— so that those having reached total salvation, the highest perfection, the ultimate goal, would be the ones who will "see" in the most complete fashion imaginable. It is well known how firmly just such is asserted in the traditional images of eternal bliss. It almost appears as if those who set out to describe the ultimate perfection could speak of nothing else but of "seeing". "What do those not see, who see the One who sees everything!"[10] "Our total reward: to see."[11] "Will not he alone, who beholds the divine in beauty, find life worth living, while he in turn is beloved by God and removed from death?"[12] "Where *theoria* succeeds, happiness succeeds."[13] "This is life eternal: to know you . . ."[14] This chorus, in which Christianity's sacred book and the theology flowing from it are in harmony with the philosophers of old, could easily be augmented by many more voices.

It should be emphasized here that all these statements

[9] Ibid., 25.

[10] "Quid est quod non videant qui videntem omnia vident?" Gregory the Great, quoted by Thomas Aquinas, *Quaestiones disputatae de veritate* 2, 2.

[11] "Tota merces nostra visio est." Augustine *Sermones* 302. Migne, *Patrologia Latina* 39, 2324; cf. also *De Trinitate* 1, 9.

[12] Plato *Symposium* 212.

[13] W. Szilasi, *Macht und Ohnmacht des Geistes* (Freiburg im Breisgau, 1947), 154. This statement is meant as an interpretation of Aristotle.

[14] Jn 17:3.

do not only aim at something "beyond" and eschatological. On the contrary, they assert that man, immersed in this world and its historical reality, desires above all to know and to see, a desire that pervades his entire existential nature. "We value nothing more than this: to see."[15] The author of this statement, Aristotle, even considers the common popular curiosity clearly as related to the philosophical *theoria*: since we are willing to travel to Olympia, regardless of the expenses involved, for no other reason than to watch some games, competitions, and entertainment, should it not be presumed that we desire all the more to contemplate *being* itself and truth?[16]

Do not worry, I have no intention to make the philosophical *theoria* and the *visio beatifica* [beatific vision] into one and the same thing. The reflection on the whole of reality and its ultimate meaning, an endeavor properly called "philosophy", proceeds rather through inquiry than through contemplation. Still, we are discussing here the reason why philosophy should be considered "meaningful in itself". Put in such a context there exists indeed some correlation. Nowhere else, it seems, does the energy of spiritual existence itself, does the hunger for unrestricted and complete participation in life—a yearning to be ultimately and ineffably satisfied only in the *visio beatifica*—never and nowhere, then, does this yearning manifest itself more plainly and more courageously, as it were, than in the simplicity of the philosophical inquiry, which concentrates, not unlike the beatific vision, on one thing only: on truth, that is, on the revelation of the everlasting object.

[15] Aristotle *Metaphysics* 1, 1:980a 25.
[16] Aristotle *Fragment* 58 (Valentin Rose).

This object of philosophy—*secondly*—we shall now discuss; more specifically: we shall discuss the particular correlation between this object and the nature of the human spirit as such.

Nowadays if we consult the appropriate manuals and dictionaries regarding the characteristics that distinguish spirit-endowed beings from those not so endowed, we will rarely find, which is indicative, one special quality that Western tradition apparently considered of even greater importance than "immateriality" or "consciousness". I am speaking of the spirit's universality as essential to its very nature: the spiritual soul, in a certain sense, is itself "the universe", *quodammodo omnia*,[17] and from the beginning designed to "correspond to all that exists", *convenire cum omni ente*.[18] This power and potency to relate to absolutely everything that exists cannot even be called—strictly speaking—a quality, something that the spirit would "possess": the spirit itself *is* this potency, this relational energy oriented toward the totality of all things.

This, then, not to be confined, nor indeed to be accommodated to the partial setting of a "habitat", but to be oriented toward *the* world of everything that is real; to exist facing the universe of all there is—this constitutes the essential nature of the spirit; this defines its superiority over all nonspiritual beings; this distinguishes, for instance, humans from animals. This very same totality of all *being* is the object also of the philosophical *theoria*. To philosophize means nothing else but to reflect on the *whole* of all reality.

Still, something seems to be amiss here. When reading

[17] Aristotle *De anima* 3, 8:431b; quoted by Thomas Aquinas, *Quaestiones disputatae de veritate* 1, 1.
[18] Aquinas, ibid.

the last few sentences, at least, some misgivings seem to arise and persist. Do we not speak here about man in terms somewhat too grand, and consequently in terms too grand also about the prospects of philosophy? There are indeed good reasons for such second thoughts. Still, these reservations are not entirely justified.

Man, of course, is not yet completely defined by calling him a spiritual ("spirit-endowed") being. More precisely, he is at the same time a bodily being in so fundamental a sense as to force us even to declare that there is nothing "purely spiritual" in man (yet nothing "purely material" either). Consequently, he is in reality incapable of living, directly and constantly, "face to face with all that exists". To satisfy physical hunger alone he needs to return to the narrow confines of his "habitat", where his search is limited, not at all surprisingly, to things useful and suitable, things necessary "to make a living". All the same, this remains true: should such confinement (to the area of economic planning, of mere concern for the daily bread, of "servile" labor and so forth) become permanent so that it can no longer be interrupted, for whatever reasons, then it incurs the danger of turning human existence, from this moment on, into something inhuman. Man indeed makes his home in this world, as is his task and his nature. And yet, it is incumbent on him, and he himself must embrace this responsibility, to actualize, every so often and in every unregimented way, the inborn potency of his spirit, and to allow himself to be challenged and disquieted in his retreat into the hassle of his workaday activities (in spite of all moaning about "rush hour" and "rat race" still a protective and even comfortable retreat). Only then will he behold, in wonder, the true dimension of "his" world, which indeed is nothing less than—everything. This precisely makes the philosophical endeavor necessary and noble and "meaningful in itself".

The "whole of reality" will, of course, not always and explicitly be made the formal object. The philosopher nonetheless is invariably occupied with it, with the universal totality of the very same world that notably is also the concern of all everyday pursuits. The well-known statement in Aristotle's *Metaphysics,* a statement perhaps too readily accepted, that the philosopher considers *"being* insofar as it is *being"*,[19] has a twofold meaning. It says, first, that the philosophical reflection on being does not deal with something "different" from all those things in front of everybody's eyes, that is, it deals with real objects and with reality. But the second thought is rather odd: what lies before everybody's eyes would be considered "insofar as" it is part of reality. One may ask, "as" what else should it be considered? And yet, such mode of reflection is in fact most unlikely to occur in this our world. The fountain pen I use for writing, for example, is seen by everybody without fail "as" this specific writing tool in common use nowadays. The question as to what it is I hold in my hand invites the expected answer detailing the specific qualities of this fountain pen, perhaps its capacity, its brand, its origin. Should I answer instead in this vein: I am holding here, don't you see, an industrial product, something invented and made by man—a *res artificialis* [a thing made by human arts], in the words of the ancients—this would be, to put it mildly, a rather unexpected reply. It would be, however, entirely to the point; even more, it would bring out certain points eminently wor-

[19] Aristotle *Metaphysics* 3, 2:1003a 21.

thy of reflection. Still, one does not commonly consider "as" *res artificialis* either a fountain pen or any other of the countless technical (or artistic) products we constantly use. Had I wanted to vex the questioner even more, I might have said something like, "This is a segment of matter". The resulting wondering thoughts in his mind can be imagined. This answer, too, would have been eminently meaningful and difficult to plumb in all its dimensions. Nevertheless, I still would not have considered and defined this my writing utensil *as something real*. I only might have provoked ridicule and laughter—which, in turn, may have reminded me of the story about the Thracian maidservant. "You don't say! This is something real?" All the same, perhaps nobody would outrightly deny this to be at least some kind of a correct answer, though a poor one; but—is it not really an answer "signifying nothing"?

The philosophers of old, on the other hand, do find expressed in this statement many things—things, by the way, that they assert are already everybody's thoughts and knowledge, only here explicitly articulated and interpreted. Expressed, they say, is for instance: that there is a "something" manifesting the activity of "being", an *ens* (present participle of *esse,* to be); at the same time this is also "something" of such and such a kind, a *res,* defined by an *ensemble de qualités*[20] [a set of qualities]; further, that it is an *aliquid,* meaning something having a definite form and thus being differentiated and—through the limits of its individuality— separated from everything else. And all of this is but the outline of a tentative first step in the direction of

[20] J. P. Sartre describes with this the concept of *essentia. L'existential-isme est un humanisme* (Paris, 1946), 18.

an answer, it is but the distant echo of an answer to the question, "What does this mean: *something real?*"

No matter what form this answer assumes in particular—the question itself has inadvertently turned into a philosophical question, and no longer does it center only on this concrete thing that at first gave rise to it. Suddenly, even though it may not be expressed explicitly, we are dealing with the structure of reality as such, the structure of everything that exists.

Alfred North Whitehead, notably referring to Plato,[21] asserted that the true problem facing the philosopher is "to conceive a complete fact".[22] As soon, however, as someone sets out to pursue this, to comprehend *completely*—say, the entirely observable fact and after all not infrequent occurrence of "death", and to define what happens when a man dies, not only as regards the physiological and biographical aspect but its entire reality—this very instant, I contend, he is no longer concerned with this specific event but rather—whether openly or implied, so declared or not—he is concerned with the universal interwovenness of all human existence, therefore with the totality of all that is, with "God and the world". And consequently, he has turned into a philosopher, and is then essentially different (again: whether he is aware of it and welcomes it, or not) from the scientist who by definition approaches his object under a clearly specified and particular aspect, and who therefore has no business talking about "God and the world". To talk this way would be as unscientific as it would be unphilosophical *not* to do so.

As the question, first prompted by something quite

[21] Plato *Sophistes* 248e.

[22] Alfred North Whitehead, *Adventures of Ideas* (New York, 1956), 203.

concrete, changes slowly or suddenly into a philosophical question, there occurs a movement involving several
dimensions. Not only do we move away ever more
from considering any "practical" aspects, as illustrated
by the example of the fountain pen; we also see at the
same time the horizon of our questioning extended to
a point where its limits are no longer discernible. Our
question, above all, becomes all the more unanswerable,
the more it involves the totality of all there is and its
meaning.

VI

If then the philosophical question must remain unanswerable—does this not mean that its object is beyond our cognition? And would it still make sense to pursue this question?

Plato's *Symposium* has Diotima declare, "None of the gods philosophizes",[1] which means that perfect knowledge and philosophy are mutually exclusive. Aristotle, in the entirely unmythical style of his *Metaphysics,* expresses obviously the same thought. The philosophical question, he says ("What is the meaning of 'being'?" What is this: something real?), has been asked "since time immemorial", and remains "in our own days, and for ever".[2] Thomas Aquinas, too, wrote an amazing statement on this (amazing because it is not found in Kant's *Critique of Pure Reason* but in the *Quaestiones disputatae* by this great teacher of Christianity whom some wanted to make into a rationalist with an answer to every possible question). *Rerum essentiae sunt nobis ignotae,*[3] the essence of a thing remains unknown to us.

[1] Plato *Symposium* 204a.

[2] Aristotle *Metaphysics* 7, 1:102b 2ff.

[3] Aquinas, *Quaestiones disputatae de veritate* 10, 1. Similarly the commentary on Aristotle's *De anima* 1, 1, no. 15; *Quaestiones disputatae de spiritualibus creaturis* 11 ad 3; *Quaestiones disputatae de veritate* 4, 1 ad 8.

How can it be, then, that the philosopher is characterized by his quest for just this: the fundamental essence of all things and even of the world as such? The same paradox is already hidden in the etymology of the very term *philosophia;* since earliest times, and especially in earliest times, the message implied in this has been clearly noticed and specifically stated (by Pythagoras, for example, and by Plato).[4] The term's meaning is mainly twofold. *First:* "philosophy" is primarily really a negative term, explicitly expressing the *absence* of wisdom. Nobody, this is implied, at least no human being, could ever possess the ultimate and unlimited knowledge of those things whose knowledge would make us fully "knowing" and "wise". The *second* dimension in the etymology of the term *philosophia,* however, brings out a quite positive character. To persevere in the quest, to continue the "loving" search for all things worthy to be known, the search for the wisdom that would be total and perfect—to persist in spite of the awareness that the ultimate, finally satisfying answer remains ever elusive: this precisely would mark the true philosopher!

But does all this not sound boldly yet tragically absurd? I do not think so. As it is, nobody can convince me that this characterization of philosophy and its object is not an entirely dispassionate and correct description of fact, a description to be given in this and no other way.

Regarding the "unknowable" object pursued by the philosopher, however, a more precise definition is needed. "Unknowable" can have several meanings; only one of them, of course, applies here.

In saying, "the stars are invisible by day", you do not comment, in a strict sense, on any characteristic

---

[4] Plato *Phaedrus* 278d.

of the stars themselves but on the conditions required for our eyes to perceive them. Nobody would deny that "by themselves" they are as visible by day as they are by night. As potential objects of visual perception they remain unchanged. Yet "invisibility" can also point to a quality of the object and mean that the object as such and in itself cannot be perceived by the human eye; a stirring of emotions is invisible in this sense, or else, a melody. If we assert, therefore, that the object of the philosophical *theoria* is "unknowable", we have to clarify whether we mean the possibilities and conditions of our (subjective) power of cognition, or else the nature of the object itself.

The difference between cognition (*cognoscere*) and understanding (*comprehendere*) should equally be clarified from the start. Understanding itself, of course, is a particular form of cognition; this especially is our concern here after all. We might say that every *understanding cognition* is the same as perfect cognition, "knowing all about it". Thomas Aquinas, it seems to me, offers an even more precise formulation: to *understand* a thing would mean, "to know it to the full extent of its essential knowability".[5] An object, therefore, is being *understood* whenever on its part there remains nothing that is merely knowable and not yet transformed into knowledge. If such a remainder is there—would we not have to call it "knowable", even though in fact it is not known? Or could there possibly exist realities, facts, relationships, and structures that "in themselves" are not knowable, not merely unknown to man as a matter of fact,

[5] "Comprehendere autem proprie dicitur aliquis aliquam rem cognoscendo, qui cognoscit rem illam quantum in se cognoscibilis est." Thomas Aquinas, *Expositio in evangelium Joannis* 1, 11.

but simply beyond human cognition as such, in the same way a melody is entirely outside the grasp of human vision?

It cannot be easily overlooked that this question involves certain fundamental convictions, certain root attitudes. Anybody trying to give an answer will soon realize that he has to declare himself as to his ultimate position. Once again, or ever still, we are dealing with the hub of the wheel where all the parts are joined together. This does not simply mean that the answer can in no wise be justified empirically—the answer discussed here, that is, which contends there are indeed no objects unknowable "in themselves", either in philosophy or anywhere else. Rather, that reality, so far as its own nature is concerned, is accessible to cognition in all its realms and structures. Such accessibility could then be called many different names: openness, disclosure, perceptibility, transparency, lucidity. "The very reality of a thing is also its inner light."[6]

Then, too, the dictum of the "truth" of all things (*omne ens est verum*) has to be called back from oblivion; for it expresses nothing else but this: everything that has *being* is by its very nature—which means, by reason of its being *real*—also knowable. Still, we are not entirely correct in saying, the statement expresses "nothing else". The "something else" it expresses is in truth even more important. This "something else" is the *reason why* all things are recognized and defined as knowable. The reason is this: all existing things originated in the creative and inventive mind of God, and *consequently,* when they

[6] "Ipsa actualitas rei est quoddam lumen ipsius", Thomas Aquinas, *In librum de causis expositio,* 6.

were conceived and then also "spoken",[7] they received in themselves, as their essence, the quality of a "spoken word",[8] the character, therefore, to be in principle understandable and intelligible. "We see all things because they exist; yet they exist because you [O God] see them."[9]

All this, one might object, is not precisely "empirical". Indeed! And it is obvious that nobody could be imposed upon to accept this world view; such things are being decided in a different arena. But it should be quite evident that the dictum about the truth of all things will lose not only its flavor but its entire meaning as soon as it is separated from the notion of the universe as creation. Such a separation precisely has been undertaken in all modern forms of rationalism, including Neo-Scholastic systematic philosophy. Nobody should be in the least surprised, therefore, that even the pitiable remains of this dictum have vanished from all living philosophizing. Yet there should be no illusion at all about this: the explicit denial of the world as creation carries with it vast consequences, also as regards the philosophical conception of reality. Such consequences may appear perhaps only little by little. This denial means not only a break with the sacred tradition of Christianity, but also with the ontological teachings of the great Greek thinkers,[10] which really means a break with the roots that inevitably determine one's own

[7] Cf. Josef Pieper, "Was heisst 'Gott spricht'?" *Catholica* 19 (1965): 189f.

[8] R. Guardini, *Welt und Person* (Würzburg, 1940), 110.

[9] Augustine *Confessiones* 13, 38; similarly 7, 4.

[10] Cf. Josef Pieper, *Über die platonischen Mythen* (Munich, 1965), 53ff.

thinking down to the formulation of one's philosophical question and all related verbal expressions. It can be argued, of course, whether this denial would indeed render even the mere notion of a "human nature" irrelevant, as none other than Jean-Paul Sartre asserts.[11] Yet it is obviously impossible to deny categorically, on the one hand, the rootedness of all things in the thought of an inventive and creative Mind, and on the other hand to take for granted, and to explain as if nothing had happened, the empirically manifested fact of the knowability of these very same things.

Do we, however, really experience *empirically* the knowability of all that is? The logician Heinrich Scholz, shortly before his death, put the following question to me, certainly not without some critical and ironical overtones: Would the heavens truly fall if *non omne ens est verum,* if it should turn out, on the contrary, that within this *ens,* within *being,* by its very structure, there would be "obscure" and unreachable realities?

Are we able, I replied, to conceive, say, of "structure" at all without *eo ipso* [by doing so] also conceiving of something that somehow would be reachable and knowable, regardless of any complexities involved, be they even infinite? Something that is real and at the same time not identifiable in principle—this not only goes beyond our conception but destroys it.

Still, he said, modern physics has obviously encountered just such cases!

I asked in response whether in those cases all further research had definitively been terminated and abandoned.

[11] "Il n'y a pas de nature humaine, puisqu'il n'y a pas de Dieu pour la concevoir." J. P. Sartre, *L'Existentialisme,* 22.

76

Indeed not, naturally!

How come this should be "naturally" so, except one is convinced, perhaps in contradiction to one's own philosophical thesis, that realities unknowable "in and by themselves" do not exist?

The dictum *omne ens est verum* may very well be expressed in this way: it makes sense to press on with research.

This very same assertion is also a tenet of orthodox Marxism, as is well known. "The world and its structure are indeed knowable"; there are "no unknowable things, rather things still unknown". These are statements found in Stalin's programmatic essay, "Dialectical and Historical Materialism";[12] and since they can claim the authority of Engels and Lenin they should not have lost anything of their official status. Do they perchance express the same notion as the ancient statement of the truth of all that is real? If not—where is the difference? The difference lies mainly in this: Stalin, to be precise, does not speak—first—about a quality of things but about the power of human cognition (even though those two aspects cannot entirely be separated one from the other). And second, as regards human reason, its power to "know the world completely"[13] is asserted citing as argument the "praxis", "experiment and manufacturing": there is nothing in this world that man could not possibly produce as well. This idea is, of course, by no means limited to Marxism alone; there is only a short step to Sartre's thesis that man himself is equally

[12] Joseph Stalin, *Über dialektischen und historischen Materialismus. Vollständiger Text und kritischer Kommentar von Iring Fetscher*, 4th ed. (Frankfurt, Berlin, Bonn, 1957), 80f. Cf. also note 8 in chapter 1 above.

[13] Cf. Engels, *Ludwig Feuerbach*, 17f.

nothing but what he makes of himself.[14] I do not dispute that in the technical and artistic area, and even as regards morals and history, there do exist "creative" activities by man—as long as we do not forget that man has never accomplished more than the reshaping of already existing realities. But here we are dealing with something entirely different; we are dealing with the fundamental and unalterable difference between things made by man and things not made by man, between *res artificiales* and *res naturales,* that is: between those things that have received their identity from human ingenuity and are therefore totally knowable, and those things that have received their identity from a divine thought and are for this reason forever beyond our full comprehension; for no finite power will ever penetrate so deep as to reach the archetypes that dwell in the mind of God.

Once again it becomes obvious here how impossible it is for all true philosophical endeavor to disregard the fundamental convictions. I am not saying—be it emphasized—that any philosopher, as long as he deals with his subject "in the correct manner", would arrive with a certain necessity at one specific interpretation of reality. I do say, however, that he will eventually arrive at a point where he cannot avoid facing fundamental conceptions about the world and existence, provided he has consistently continued his philosophical quest without any preconceived ideas. This may indeed be the point as well when he sees himself compelled explicitly to accept the world view contained in the tradition, or explicitly to reject it.

The dictum, *omne ens est verum,* even its rather optimistic rendering almost in the form of a slogan belonging

---

[14] Sartre, *L'Existentialisme,* 22.

to the politics of science ("It makes sense to press on with research")—this dictum, then, shows to our surprise a double face. One face reveals all things as accessible to an ever deeper cognition, the other presents them as impossible ever to be comprehended completely. Both aspects, in fact, not only—in Fechner's words—the "daytime view" but also the "nighttime view", the inexhaustible depth of all reality—both aspects can be experienced empirically. And yet, the notion that both spring from the same root, that both are—in a certain sense—even identical; that, more specifically, all things in themselves are entirely knowable because they originate in the infinite *lucidity* of the divine Logos, and that they are, nevertheless, inexhaustible for us because they originate, once again, in the *infinite* lucidity of the divine Logos—this, of course, lies beyond all empirical demonstration.

On the dividing line, where the knowable and the inexhaustible aspects touch, there the philosophical act occurs; it is triggered by the awareness that world and existence are indeed beyond our full comprehension.

This dividing line, incidentally, is not defined once and for all. It cannot be determined, *in concreto,* where exactly it is situated. Moreover, depending on the greater or lesser openness and clarifying energy of the individual mind, it can seemingly be pushed farther ahead in a way not definable from the start. In this we find again one of the differences between science and philosophy: in philosophy the individual person and his power of cognition carry incomparably more weight. It makes sense to speak of "science" as one multifaceted endeavor throughout the centuries, almost using it as a collective term. "Science has determined . . ."—it is entirely justified to talk this way. It is meaningless, on the other hand, to declare that "philosophy" has discovered or explained this or that. As much as a living philosophy "happens" in the dialogue among different minds, even *as* dialogue: there can nonetheless be no teamwork in philosophy. No philosopher can in any way use the "results" of Plato's philosophy, except if he repeats, by and for himself, Plato's thinking. In the realm of science, in contrast, the results achieved by an individual researcher can be used by anybody without the need to repeat the scientific journey of this individual.

Philosophy, above all, does not work in a way that the more a subject matter is explored, the more those "white areas on the map" would diminish and disappear. On the contrary: this image, entirely appropriate for the scientific exploration of the world, applies in almost the opposite sense: the more penetrating and comprehensive the insight, the more overwhelming becomes the awareness of the vast field of what remains unknown. This, of course, is so because of the infinite dimension of the blueprint that the philosopher, through his philosophy, sets out to decipher.

With regard to the possibility, then, of answering the philosophical question and determining its object as knowable or unknowable, we may state, in short, the following: it may well happen that the philosopher's unbiased approach is compromised, or that his mental energy slackens and disintegrates. Still, on his journey two things can never happen: he will never encounter a limit inherent in his object as such, a limit that would simply prevent him from pressing on farther. Nor will he ever arrive at the end of his journey, that is, at a point where the question that had impelled him onward would be answered once and for all.

The world view on which these assertions are based

and which alone renders them plausible, stands by its very nature in opposition against two fronts: against all forms of agnostic resignation, and against all rationalist arrogance. Both have, far beyond the departmental realm of philosophy, greatest contemporary import. This same world view, strangely enough, stands every now and then in danger of being mistaken for the positions of its adversaries, even of turning itself into these positions. The only safeguard against this happening consists in the awareness that, on the one hand, we are confronted with an unfathomable reality, yet the unfathomable reality of a world perfectly "lucid" in and by itself; and that, on the other hand, there is universal knowability, yet the knowability of a world illuminated by an "inaccessible light".

VII

Karl Jaspers, in an academic address in 1960, made the statement that philosophy "has become an embarrassment for everybody."[1] He did not mean philosophy's natural outsider status in relation to a world where usefulness and practicality reign supreme, but rather the situation of philosophy within the realm of the contemporary university. To eliminate this embarrassment, it seems to me, you would have to eliminate at the same time philosophy itself. We are faced here, put in provisional terms, with an equally natural incommensurability, namely, that between scientific and philsophical thinking. What else should we expect, other than an ever more pronounced incommensurability, the more exclusively our universities submit to the standards of the exact sciences? The tendency toward such an exclusive attitude, evident to everybody, has of course its good reasons; it is all but inevitable. Philosophy, in contrast, proceeds in a way that is indeed, by scientific standards, offensive, even impossible—provided we mean by "philosophy" the same that Plato, Aristotle, and the great philosophical tradition up to Karl Jaspers meant.

Nevertheless, scientific research and philosophy in

[1] Karl Jaspers, *Wahrheit und Wissenschaft* (Basel, 1960), 20.

themselves have never been one another's real enemies. A closer look shows it is not they that are the two sides in the dispute going on, true, for quite some time and for everybody to see. The vocal participants in this controversy are rather those who declare the exact sciences to be the one and only and obligatory standard and norm for all serious consideration of reality and truth. In this, however, they advance a thesis obviously not of the specifically scientific domain but pertaining to the theory of science, and therefore a philosophical thesis. In fact, this is the widespread explicit claim, for example, by the proponents of a "scientific philosophy". And on the other side? The one so attacked does not, of course, deny the sovereignty of the scientific domain. Yet he insists that there are other forms of cognitive quest, certainly correlated to science in various ways, even dependent on it, and nonetheless distinct and equally indispensable—for example: philosophy.

Such controversies are usually not the results of irrelevant or irresponsible whims. We should rather expect them to be connected with certain changes in the total historical structure of human existence. This necessitates from time to time a revision and redefinition of the respective positions. In no way does it mean that such conflicts would basically be nothing more than misunderstandings solvable through better explanations. Definitely not! On the contrary, some disagreements will stand out all the more sharply after more detailed clarification. It is, of course, impossible to specify here the principles of scientific research and, on the other hand, spell out in detail what it means to philosophize. Still, to draw up some kind of inventory concerning the main grievances shall nonetheless be attempted here, at least a brief identification of the "differences" (in a double sense) that quite regularly and predictably trigger the polemic.

First and foremost, we have to recall the image of the unending trail that I have employed, quite tentatively, to characterize the internal situation of the philosopher. This analogy applies much more specifically than may have appeared at first. Above all, it points to the most fundamental difference separating philosophy from scientific research. True, science has on occasion also been described as "reaching out to ever new horizons", but this is not the same.

The physicist, tackling a problem confronting him, does not at all set out on an infinite journey. There comes the moment, though perhaps only after a very long time, when he reaches the goal. At that point, the question is answered, the hope held out is fulfilled, the aim is realized. There may arise immediately further questions; but this will then present a new task. He who endeavors to reflect on the totality of world and existence, that is, to philosophize, sets foot on a path that in this life will never come to an end. He will always remain "on the way", the question will never receive an answer once and for all, the hope will never find fulfillment. He may perhaps succeed in explaining to someone, more or less convincingly, that in this way, through the living pursuit of the question and the hope, at least an openness for the infinite object, the whole of reality, is sustained. This object is thus constantly chased after and aimed at, as otherwise its existence might simply be forgotten. Still, this constitutes an exceedingly upsetting and unbearable manner of speaking, not so much for the scientist as rather for the "scientific world view": we do "not acknowledge any unsolvable riddles";[2] "all our knowledge of reality is gained strictly through the techniques of the different scientific disciplines; any other 'ontology' is so much empty talk."[3] In short, making precision and perfection into absolutes on the one hand, and accepting a preliminary "not-yet" on the other—these two approaches are mutually exclusive; nothing could be clearer than that.

There is now, as is well known, the "ancient utterance" that describes man himself, all in all, as ever unfinished and "on his way", the *viator,* the wanderer—no matter how many particular journeys he may complete and how much else he may accomplish in terms of knowledge and practical or creative activity. Existence itself would therefore be structured on hope—in the same way as philosophy. Indeed, I wonder whether you first have to acknowledge and to accept this admittedly quite vague connection between the intrinsic structure of existence and the philosophical act before you can at all conceive of this philosophical act as the mind's attention, in search and hope, to the mystery of the world—not merely as something "quite possible" but as something that man cannot ignore nor do without.

One other persistent controversy between philosophy and science centers on the radically different concept of what constitutes a greater or lesser perfection in human knowledge. The position taken by science will probably be: knowledge is in the same measure perfect as it succeeds in capturing an instance of reality, no matter what kind, through clear concepts and precise

[2] *Wissenschaftliche Weltauffassung,* 15.

[3] M. Schlick, "Erleben, Erkennen, Metaphysik", *Kant-Studien* 31 (1926): 157.

description. The philosopher, in contrast, regardless of how deeply he may be impressed by the formal perfection of scientific thinking, remains for his part quite unable to acknowledge in this quality the perfection of knowledge as such.

Let me relate an event that for me is not only a touching testimony but also a telling fact bearing on our topic here. Alfred North Whitehead, whose career had begun under the auspices of the *Principia Mathematica*,[4] a work of such extremely formalized exactness that it might be fully comprehended and grasped by only a few, toward the end of his life had come to philosophize with the breadth and depth of the great Western tradition. He could therefore claim greater legitimacy than anybody else when toward the end he declared, "The exactness is a fake", an illusion, a phantom. This is the closing sentence of his farewell lecture at age eighty (on the topic of "immortality"), given at Harvard University in the spring of 1941.[5] Nathaniel Lawrence, who authored a fundamental study on Whitehead's philosophical development,[6] was present at this memorable lecture; he told me how Whitehead spoke this, his last public statement, "with all the energy that his high-pitched, raspy voice would yield, and with such radiant kindness as to suggest he was about to say, 'The Lord is my Shepherd'; and maybe this is what indeed was

[4] This is the title of a three-volume work, with Bertrand Russell as coauthor, which has become a standard text of modern mathematical logic; it appeared 1910–13.

[5] A. N. Whitehead, "Immortality", the Ingersoll lecture at Harvard Divinity School, given on April 22, 1941, and printed in *The Philosophy of A. N. Whitehead,* ed. P. A. Schilpp (New York, 1951), 700.

[6] Nathaniel Lawrence, *Whitehead's Philosophical Development* (University of California Press, 1956).

on his mind". There can be not even the shadow of a suspicion that this statement would have been intended to advocate or merely acknowledge any form of irrationalism. What it reveals, on the contrary, is a transformed concept of perfection in human cognition, a concept no longer dictated by science; in brief: the philosophical concept.

It has already been mentioned that being "critical", for the philosopher, means diligently taking care not to ignore anything. Yet the whole of reality, which is the object of such care, is not the same as the sum total resulting from adding up each and every thing. Rather it means the *totum,* the ordered structure of the world, containing a hierarchy, greater and lesser actualizations of *being,* and above all a highest reality that at the same time is the most profound foundation and origin of everything, of every single thing and of the whole as well. I am well aware that this, so far, is no more than my assertion, and a rather audacious and "unsecured" assertion at that, standing in dire need of some justification. Still, this is not the place to discuss it further, much less to prove its validity. Here I wanted only to show why he who reflects on reality as such, the philosopher, will necessarily have a concept of "perfect knowledge" different from that held by the individual sciences, and also that for him knowledge is perfect inasmuch as reality is contemplated in its totality and in its foremost manifestations. Decisive in this is the ontological rank of what is perceived, not the *modus* of how it is perceived.

The principle of scientific exactness, in turn, by itself does not enable us to distinguish between things on an ontologically "higher" or "lower" level, not even between knowledge more beneficial for us or less. It does not allow such distinction, it rather prevents it. Still, this is entirely as it should be; it should not be held against it. The situation becomes deplorable only when those distinctions, judged from a position that grants the principle of scientific exactness absolute status, are generally declared impossible or simply meaningless. T. S. Eliot relates how the beginnings of his philosophical studies had been overshadowed by a feeling of inferiority with regard to the exact sciences, and he mentions, incidentally, also the *Principia Mathematica*. Since then, he adds, he looks at this overemphasis on formal exactness in philosophy and finds an analogy in certain contemporary approaches to the fine arts: the latter offer the possibility of producing "works of art without imagination", while the former provides "a method of philosophizing" in which "insight and wisdom" seem equally dispensable.[7]

Only out of the soil of "loving pursuit of wisdom", indeed of true *philo-sophia,* could this be said: "The smallest amount of knowledge about the most sublime realities is more desirable than the most perfect knowledge about the lowest things"; "though we may hardly touch the things supreme and divine, their knowledge is nonetheless more important to us than all the things of this our world together; just as it is so much sweeter to catch but a glimpse, however fleeting, of the beloved than to have exact knowledge of many other, even important, things." The first of these quotations is found in the *Summa theologica* of Thomas Aquinas.[8] The author of the second statement is Aristotle[9] whose usually

[7] T. S. Eliot, preface to Josef Pieper, *Leisure, the Basis of Culture* 7th ed. (London and New York, 1964).

[8] Thomas Aquinas, *Summa theologica* I, 1, 5 ad 1.

[9] Aristotle *De partibus animalium* 1, 5:644bff.

dispassionate prose may not have led you to expect such courtly language from him.

"Philosophy does not result in 'philosophical propositions', but rather in the clarification of propositions."[10] This thesis, found in Ludwig Wittgenstein's *Tractatus Logico-Philosophicus,* also intends to define one of the fundamental differences between philosophy and science. It shall be left open here whether or not Wittgenstein meant to say, as seems likely, that the task of philosophy consists mainly, or even exclusively, in the logical clarification of those statements through which science expresses its findings. All the same, the assertion as formulated expresses indeed, perhaps even beyond the intention of its author, an essential characteristic of philosophy, a characteristic that is bound to appear, when measured with the principle of scientific exactness, once again as implausible and even as somewhat scandalous.

All achievements of science are basically discoveries, that is, they bring into the open what until then has been hidden and unknown. In this sense to explore the world—this is the glory of the sciences! Such glory can obviously not be claimed by the philosopher, and thus the verdict seems rendered already. The remarkable thing here is, however, that in philosophy this very "defect" is specifically singled out and made into an element of philosophy's self-understanding. Philosophy, as we say, is in fact aiming at something totally other than the increase of our knowledge of the world. What else might this be? A tentative answer could be: it is the re-calling of knowledge already present yet forgotten, which must not remain forgotten.

[10] Ludwig Wittgenstein, *Tractatus Logico-Philosophicus,* 5th ed. (London, 1951), 4, 112.

He who reflects as a philosopher, that is, under every possible aspect, on realities such as guilt, freedom, or death; or he who considers the fundamental question as to the structure of *being* ("What does it mean for something to be real?"), will certainly experience a progressively more profound insight into all that is, in the same measure as his cognitive analysis penetrates ever deeper, and as his mind opens up ever more in dispassionate and receptive readiness. More profound insight, of course, is the philosopher's aim. Still, properly speaking, we cannot maintain that the philosopher, through this approach, would discover things totally unknown thus far, totally unthought thus far, things altogether new and original. What happens is rather a process resembling the illumination of something already vaguely and darkly known, the conquest of something almost lost in oblivion, indeed the regaining of what had been forgotten, which is called "remembrance". Even the truly "new" achievements of the masters—say, Aristotle's discovery that contrary to Parmenides' opinion there does exist between *being* and *nothing* a third level, the level of possibilities and becoming, the level of readiness for actualization, called *potentia* (*dynamis*)—even such an insight, never before explicitly conceived and expressed, could be accepted and acknowledged as valid not as a result of a comparison with empirical and verifiable facts, but only because of a renewed cognition *in remembrance*. This is the rule in the philosophical endeavor: something already known, "by nature and implicitly", is transformed through a "secondary effort" —secondary with respect to this primary awareness— into reflective and explicit cognition.[11]

---

[11] Caspar Nink, *Ontologie. Versuch einer Grundlegung* (Freiburg im Breisgau, 1952), 6f.

This is perforce quite unimpressive when compared to the triumphs of the sciences, which every day present something new in terms of facts, structures, and inter-connections—bringing all this before people's eyes, and even more so into people's hands: first of all ever more perfect means, scientifically tested, of domination over nature. The philosopher and philosophy, in contrast—do they not deal with the same topics all the time? Do they not discuss perpetually the same problems? Objections of this kind have been raised already against Socrates; Alcibiades mentions this is Plato's *Symposium*.[12] And how is it with progress in philosophy? Does it exist at all? Such questions can without doubt be construed in a context of complete contempt, a contempt that indeed is heaped, every so often, on those who engage in philosophy; a contempt that is justified if the rule of scientific exactness by right possesses or demands absolute authority.

But then, it shall be conceded right away: "progress" in the philosophical realm is assuredly a problematic category—insofar as it means an ever growing collective accumulation of knowledge, growing in the same measure as time passes. There exists, under this aspect, an analogy to poetry. Has Goethe "progressed" farther than Homer?—one cannot ask such a question. Philosophical progress undeniably occurs, yet not so much in the succession of generations as rather in the personal and dynamic existence of the philosopher himself, indeed to the extent to which he is able to behold, in silence and openness, the full depth and extension of his proper object, which is ever new and at the same time so very ancient.

How little opposition there is in principle between

---

[12] Plato *Symposium* 221e.

the sciences themselves in their own domain and the philosophical quest has rarely been more evident than in our own time. The scientific exploration of reality nowadays seems to have reached, in certain fields at any rate, such an advanced frontier as to be almost identical with the approach of the philosopher. And as long as the interest remains fixed, without bias, on all that can be perceived, this approach is usually adopted without hesitation. Thus it may happen that the *nuclear physicist,* for instance, in his search for the elementary structure of matter and remaining strictly within the domain of physics, comes finally so close to the philosophical question, "What is, after all and in its core, the reality of matter?", that the dividing line between physics and philosophy seems to have vanished. Finding among contemporary nuclear physicists not a few who felt compelled to make statements that properly belong in philosophy, could find its explanation in part in just such a particular experience. The researcher in the empirical *psychoanalytical* field, too, usually encounters existential conditions of such kind as to confront him, the moment he attempts to interpret his "results", with the unavoidable question about the ultimate meaning of human life. Even the *homo faber* ["man the maker"], through all his scientific practicalities, has from time to time been pushed into a situation where the borderline in question also appears. This happens, for instance, whenever the perpetual quest for the control of nature's energy reaches a point of highest success. To come face to face with the mind-boggling power given into man's hands seems to force as well the contemplation of "what this is all about". To witness this, one has only to read the documentation on the first nuclear explosion in the desert of Alamogordo. "Even the staunchest atheists were so shaken that they could describe their feelings only in religious images."[13] Robert J. Oppenheimer's remark that science at last has come face to face with sin, has been quoted countless times. And the first session of the *Atomic Energy Commission* was opened by its chairman with the concluding words of the traditional oath, as having for him, he said, a meaning like never before: "So help me God!"[14] Even should one see in all this nothing but helpless romanticism if not sentimentality, one thing cannot be denied: from one moment to the next, you are no longer dealing with the specific "sector" that is the customary and exclusive domain of science and technology. Most clearly, you are all of a sudden dealing with the totality of the world and existence!

The moment a scientist—be he a nuclear physicist, a psychoanalyst, or whatever—steps beyond these boundaries, all that has been said of the philosopher will then obviously apply to him as well. The questions then faced cannot be answered any more with the same exactitude that just a moment earlier, when the specialized expert was speaking, would have been expected unreservedly. And any potential insight thus achieved, unlike scientific results, does not become our property entirely at our disposal; suddenly we realize why the ancients spoke of "a gift on loan"[15] instead. Maybe, if the quest is honest and fortunate, and since the connection between these now all-encompassing questions and one's own existence cannot be ignored any more, it may just be that a new awareness arises: that philosophy and human existence itself, both, are structured in the pattern of hope.

[13] Margret Boveri, *Der Verrat im 20. Jahrhundert,* vol. 4 (Hamburg, 1960), 205.

[14] Ibid., 206.

[15] Aquinas, *In duodecim libros* 1, 3, no. 64.

VIII

Although the claim advanced by the "scientific" world view to represent the only valid approach does not lead anywhere but into sterility, there is for the philosopher nothing more beneficial than to face this challenge head-on. It would be unfortunate if he should try to avoid the clarifying controversy and the continuous dialogue in which the comprehension of the world as well as man's self-understanding ever unfolds, and in which the exact sciences, not by accident, have a leading role nowadays. Since the scientific methods become ever more refined, it is inevitable that the critical expectations with regard to philosophy and philosophical articulation also expand. The challenge posed to the philosopher in all this, namely, to rethink his own possibilities, presents at the same time an opportunity, and to miss this opportunity would be inexcusable—if philosophy is not to disqualify itself from the *recherche collective de la vérité*[1] [the collective quest for truth], the great endeavor to "know reality".

The philosopher should be willing, I would say, to listen to "scientific" critique, even if it is mistaken, mainly in two respects: with respect to *language,* and with respect to *experience.*

[1] M. D. Chenu, *Introduction à l'étude de Saint Thomas d'Aquin* (Paris, 1950), 291.

Too many times, to be sure, has Wittgenstein's pronouncement been thrown into our faces as a warning and a reproach: "What can be said at all can be said clearly, and what we cannot talk about we must pass over in silence."[2] This aphorism, at closer scrutiny, yields much less than its pretentious tone proclaims. The rule it lays down does not inconvenience anybody for the simple reason that the preceding statement of fact is rather questionable. How can it be determined whether there is something that cannot possibly be "said at all"? Above all, what does "clearly" mean here?

Whitehead has stated, "Clarity always means 'clear enough'."[3] Clarity is not something absolute; it always means "sufficiently clear for someone". Still, "clear enough" for what? Does "saying something with clarity" mean the same as "saying something in such a wise that the subject matter appears sharply delineated and entirely distinct before our eyes"? Or do we also have to consider "clear" a statement informing us that we are dealing with a reality whose dimension is *not* fully knowable, and which therefore can never be grasped clearly and distinctly? Obviously one can still speak about a subject that cannot be fully comprehended nor adequately described, and speak in such a way as to make this impossibility itself very clear, perhaps even by indicating its degree and its reason. In just such a situation does the philosopher find himself; this precisely is his distinction, finding himself compelled to speak about things undoubtedly real yet nonetheless impossible to be described with verbal exactitude. And his specific difficulty, insofar as it lies in the area of language

[2] Wittgenstein, *Tractatus Logico-Philosophicus,* 26.
[3] Whitehead, "Remarks", 179.

at all, consists in letting this ultimate unutterable dimension, together with what is positively stated, appear in his pronouncements.

Such inherent limitations are never incumbent on the scientist—which explains more readily why he is so quick at times to criticize the language found in philosophical writings. It is a triumph all too easily gained, taking a statement by Hegel out of its context, putting it as it were in a display case, and inviting the uninformed to look critically at "the so-called philosophical language ... the way a zoologist views a rare species of an insect".[4]

This does not imply, on the other hand, that the philosopher would have nothing to learn from the language of the sciences. Even the most complicated scientific utterance does not diminish the fact that the primary purpose of language, by its very nature, aims at communicating an insight about reality. We are not talking here about a "common and ready understanding", but about the natural function of all language. Even if you take, say, Albert Einstein's later texts on the theory of relativity, which only a few are able to decipher at all and to penetrate with understanding—it is nevertheless never the language as such that makes understanding difficult. On the contrary: it is precisely the language that opens up an access to a reality in itself difficult to grasp. Everybody knows, however, that the difficulty of reading a philosophical text derives all too often from nothing else but a misuse of language, so that the very language is the obstacle, the language alone. This offends not only the scientific mind; it equally goes against the manner of thinking and speaking found in the great

[4] Reichenbach, *Aufstieg der wissenschaftlichen Philosophie*, 13, 82ff.

philosophical tradition of the West, from Plato to Nietzsche. Just think of the solid and straightforward comparisons employed by Socrates, who unconcerned about his own "importance" speaks of cobblers, of colts and calves, or else—to illustrate the concept of *idea*—of a broken loom shuttle. Not only does all this aim naturally at nothing else but precision and clarity; it also wants to facilitate—which is of course all but the same reason— the dialogue with the listener. Plato, Aristotle, Augustine, Thomas: all of them had the same basic attitude in this; they even made the use of everyday language their linguistic principle. "Name your things with the many in mind"[5] —and this not merely as a didactic device, but above all because otherwise the thinking itself would lose its cogency. Wherever, in contrast, the linguistic common ground—common because of explicit efforts or implicit convention—is replaced by an arbitrary terminology on the part of an individual, there the speaker steps outside the common realm of the human quest for knowledge. To be sure, this does not prevent the formation of fan clubs but rather fosters it. *Der Tod ist als der Schrein des Nichts das Gebirg des Seins* ["Death, as it enshrines nothingness, is the shelter of being"]—a sentence such as this is all but impossible to translate into any other language,[6] a fact not to be

---

[5] Aristotle *Topics* 2, 2:110a. Thomas Aquinas quotes this statement in his *Summa contra gentiles* 1, 1. Cf. also his *Quaestiones disputatae de veritate* 4, 2.

[6] In Kyoto, Japan, I met a university professor who had translated the author of this sentence into Japanese. I asked him how, in this context, *das Gebirg des Seins* would be rendered in translation. Since I am not acquainted with the Japanese, he answered without the slightest hesitation, "the mountain of being". It is obvious that this has nothing at all to do with the meaning of the German text. Still,

taken lightly. Yet what makes it really a disaster is not even its hazy meaning; the real disaster lies in the implicit, barely concealed attitude of considering any request for clarification an act of impertinence.

It may be the ancient notion comes to mind here that sees a kinship between philosophy and poetry. In fact, even such unromantic thinkers as Aristotle and Thomas Aquinas have mentioned this kinship; poet and philosopher, both would confront the *mirandum* [wonder].[7] Still, although this kinship naturally will also have a bearing on the language of philosophy, it does not at all imply that the philosopher would be allowed to dispense with the obligation to speak with the utmost clarity. It is, after all, obviously the common *object* that according to such a notion unites philosophy and poetry. Both direct their attention, in contrast to the practical and everyday interests, toward the realm of wonder, a realm boundlessly unfolding below the surface, and even right in the middle, of our matter-of-fact world. Not to conceal this unfathomable footing of the world, but to point to it and recall it—this precisely is the challenge posed to the language of both the philosopher and the poet. Yet the specific distinction by no

---

the question arises whether it was not, after all, the original expression that prompted such nonsensical translation. Moreover, *"A partir du jeu de miroir du Tour encerclant du Souple, le rassemblement propre à la chose se produit"*—who would ever suspect that this claims to be the translation of the following German sentence: "Aus dem Spiegel-Spiel des Gerings des Ringen ereignet sich das Dingen des Dinges" ["Out of the mirror-play of the ringing of the ring eventuates the 'thinging' of the thing"]? Cf. Martin Heidegger, *Vorträge und Aufsätze* (Pfullingen, 1954), 179; and the French edition, *Essais et Conférences,* trans. André Préau (Paris, 1958), 215.

[7] Cf. Aquinas, *In duodecim libros* 1, 3, no. 55.

means vanishes; the philosophical approach, other than in poetry, does not intend to paint a picture through experiential and sense-related formal elements (tone, rhythm, atmosphere, symbol), but tries to grasp reality in abstract concepts. The struggle, of course, to capture the unfathomable depth of *being* nonetheless in clear conceptual utterances—this constitutes, as mentioned before, the specific linguistic difficulty of all philosophy.

Clarity of the utterance, then, is indeed demanded of philosophy, just as it is of science. Yet clarity is not the same as "precision". There is, in any event, a kind of precision that as a matter of fact must remain beyond the philosopher's reach; after all, he cannot possibly even aspire to it. Now is the time to mention a certain proposal that is usually a recurring element of any "scientific" critique of philosophy. It is the proposal, generally advanced in rather apodictic terms, that the philosopher should renounce the use of the indigenous common and organic language, in favor of science's approach, creating a "symbolism cleansed from all the dross of the historical languages",[8] that is, a formalized language of symbols, an artificial terminology. The mathematical symbol and the artificial term carry indeed that specific precision establishing science as science: the explicit concentration of the investigative interest on one narrow and particular aspect. The very same reason renders any artificial and formalized language unusable in the philosophical realm. The word "precise" comes from "cut off". A term is *precise* by neatly cutting off, under a certain aspect, a partial phenomenon from a more complex reality and presenting it, as an isolated specimen, to the observer. To repeat: it is, therefore, entirely proper for science to employ its own artificial

[8] *Wissenschaftliche Weltauffassung,* 15.

terminology. In the philosophical domain, however, this would result at best in some pseudo-precision; it would rather obscure philosophy's specific topic and push it into oblivion. The natural language, in contrast, derives its vigor from the ability to keep this topic alive throughout. Physicians, for instance, on occasion use the technical term *exitus* for the physiological fact of cardiac arrest, and the term is precise. "Death", as belonging to the natural language, is not a technical term but a *word;* it is less precise, but more expressive, because "death" designates the entire spectrum of what happens when a person dies.

To be sure, in philosophy, too, especially in its auxiliary disciplines such as formal logic, it may be advisable or even necessary to employ an artificial terminology, which in this case would also be familiar only to the specialist and the expert. Within his own proper domain, however, the philosopher speaks of things that by their very nature do not concern the specialist only but every human being. His utterances are not necessarily grasped already after some superficial listening, without cost, as it were. There may result, on the contrary, serious difficulties for a full understanding, difficulties to be overcome perhaps less through the efforts of conceptual reasoning and more through meditative silence, which is not brought about, rather may be hindered, by intense mental exertion. The decisive aspect in all philosophical expression is nevertheless this: to employ diligently, not a terminology, but the elements of our common language, and thus to speak in the power, of naturally grown words already familiar to everyone, in such a way that the object of philosophy, the quest for wisdom, which is also of concern to everyone, is upheld and preserved with clarity.

Incidentally, this philosophical object may reveal its

truly unexpected reason for wonder even to those who start out by trying to describe it in the precise language of "protocol propositions". This puts it all into a new and entirely different light, a consequence that will not, however, affect those who adamantly claim that facts described in such a way are the only and total reality of the event at hand. One could, for example, put together in the manner of a research physicist the protocol sentences relative to the observable and measurable events occurring when two people shake hands. (They stand, facing each other, at a certain distance one from the other; one forearm of each, up to this point in an almost vertical position, is then raised as if through a lever action in such a way that both respective hands touch each other; each person's hand now grasps the other's hand in a mutual grip for a measurable period of time, exerting an equally measurable pressure—and so on and so forth). If anybody would observe and describe this event in such terms, *and* if he would at the same time realize and know that with this same handshake, just captured in protocol sentences, two adversaries, say, are sealing their mutual reconciliation, then he would certainly be offered, it seems to me, exciting new possibilities to experience the inexhaustible *mirandum* of our human existence.

The "scientific" critique of philosophy, besides emphasizing the lack of precision of its language, seems to look most unfavorably on its questionable relation to any empirical basis. The demand implied in this is, of course, not entirely unambiguous. Yet the observation is doubtlessly justified insofar as it points out that philosophy, like any other cognitive claim, has to legitimate itself by keeping in evidence its connection to the empirical basis. True, the philosopher, by discussing, for instance, what is implied in the concept of *being,* steps beyond the realm of empirical reality; yet this exploration, if it is not to turn into unmoored speculation and fantasy, must obviously start directly with actual or at least potential experience. At some point the reflection, of course, will center on the innermost structure of all that is real, a structure no longer in immediate evidence and also perhaps not adequately expressible in words. Still, that the discussion indeed refers to the structure of the same things lying in front of everybody's eyes—the fact and reason of this connection must be capable of being demonstrated. The following statement sounds rather aggressive and indeed that is intended: "There is no way to gain factual knowledge except the way of experience."[9] This sentence can be understood in a quite acceptable sense. It would be hopeless, at any rate, and not worth the effort to take the manifold results of mere mental speculation and construction, be they in form of essays or entire systems, and try to defend them as "philosophy".

On the other hand, it is a misunderstanding, not infrequent, to consider that statement about experience to be itself a statement from experience. This should be quite evident—if not at first sight, then at least at second sight. Whoever defends its truth, indeed, has already conceded that our basic convictions, by necessity and I suppose also by right, rest as well on realities other than experience—always including experience, of course.

But what does "experience" mean? As a preliminary answer I propose this: experience is knowledge coming from direct contact with reality. Experience, however,

[9] Ibid., 28.

happens—as few would doubt any longer—not only (though primarily) through sense perception in which things literally "tickle our senses", as the first sentence of *The Critique of Pure Reason* states.[10] We "experience" something not only at that moment when our hand touches an object or our eyes see what is visible. The whole living human body acts as an infinitely differentiated and sensitive receptacle of this direct contact with reality and thus forms one whole organ for possible experiences.

Here now, no doubt, we have one of the basic sources of all knowledge. Nothing of all that this organ perceives in its contact with reality—the external world or indeed the reality of our own selves—nothing of all this may be disregarded if we are to gain, through the "way of experience", a more comprehensive, more penetrating knowledge of all there is. Whitehead has stated this condition in almost passionate terms; nothing must be left out, everything plays a role: the experience of the one who is awake as well as the one who sleeps or is drunk or gripped by fear; experiences in light as also in darkness, in pain as also in happiness; the experience of the believer and the sceptic, even normal and abnormal experience.[11] Furthermore, he adds, these experiential findings do not at all disappear when the act of experienc-

[10] Immanuel Kant, *Kritik der reinen Vernunft,* 2nd ed., introduction.

[11] "Nothing can be omitted, experience drunk and experience sober, experience sleeping and experience waking, experience drowsy and experience wide-awake, experience self-conscious and experience self-forgetful, experience intellectual and experience physical, experience religious and experience sceptical, experience anxious and experience care-free, experience anticipatory and experience retrospective, experience happy and experience grieving, experience dominated by motion and experience under self-restraint, experience in the light and experience in the dark, experience normal and experience abnormal." Whitehead, *Adventures of Ideas,* 290f.

ing is over; they are gathered and "stored": in our great institutions; in the very behavior of people; in our language and important literary works; above all, as everybody knows, in the treasure troves of science.[12]

I insist that nothing less than all this—and perhaps even more—is included in the total body of human experience. Consequently I also accept the demand of critics that philosophy must justify itself by its foundation on experience. Such de-dogmatization and emancipation of the concept of "experience", of course, clearly establishes a challenge that, to the surprise of philosophy's positivistic critics, now turns against them.

Philosophy, on the other hand, if it is obliged to deal with so vast an experiential basis, is by this very fact all the more challenged to live up to an almost superhuman claim. How could one individual, no matter how great a genius, ever include in his philosophy the totality of all the empirical findings about the world, or at least everything known to science? The fact is that "the demands on the philosopher can never be fulfilled"[13] —this sigh of resignation by Dilthey is right on target. This demand, then, cannot be satisfied in positive terms. It can nevertheless be satisfied in a different way, by way of *not* doing something, as it were. And this form of satisfying the demand can without hesitation be expected from every philosopher: he must never formally exclude from his consideration any possible information on the realm of reality. The very moment he would do this he would cease to fulfill his proper task, which consists in the reflection on the totality of all that is real, and this from every possible angle.

[12] Ibid., 291.

[13] *Briefwechsel zwischen Wilhelm Dilthey und dem Grafen Paul Yorck v. Wartenburg 1877–1897* (Halle, 1923), 39.

IX

There is really not much disagreement in this regard: that the philosopher has to respect the findings of science. The controversy lies elsewhere. Who would dispute that nowadays anybody searching philosophically into the "essence" of man (whatever this may mean specifically) can no longer disregard that man, say, is an "evolutionary phenomenon" occupying his distinct position in the spectrum of the universe and of all life, and that according to our best knowledge he could have appeared on earth neither earlier nor later than the actual occurrence. Philosophical anthropology has indeed stated that research in the field of evolution has forced the elimination of "supposedly philosophical insights that in truth were nothing of the kind".[1] The same holds true for other applied sciences such as psychology, behavorial sciences, social sciences, and so forth. Nobody will be quick to deny that it would be entirely unphilosophical to disregard on purpose even one single scientific finding, and to declare, for instance, that for the moment the "metaphysical nature" of man alone would be of interest.

How would it be, then, should someone insist that

---

[1] Norbert Luyten, "Zum Evolutionsproblem in philosophischer Sicht", in *Naturwissenschaft und Theologie* 2 (Munich, 1959), 168.

any philosophical discussion of human nature could equally not ignore the notion of a certain consequential and fateful event having afflicted man at his primordial beginnings, something like transgression and punishment, which fundamentally marked man's historical existence up to the present day? Among those who assert such a thing we find none other than Plato. While discussing, in the *Symposium,* the question as to the ultimate meaning of Eros, a question highly relevant to anthropology, he includes without hesitation, after the contributions of psychology, sociology, and natural science, also the mythical account of man's fall, through his own doing, from an original state of complete perfection. Plato obviously holds that the philosopher has to reflect not only on all the available secular knowledge but also on the religious patrimony. In attempting "to determine exactly what makes a philosopher", the *Politeia* lists as the first characteristic "the desire for the *whole* of wisdom".[2] Any truly consuming desire, we read, is always directed toward something whole; a truly hungry person would never say, "I like this kind of food, but not that other kind".[3] Just so is the soul of the true philosopher "always poised to take hold of the whole and the totality, be it human or divine".[4]

Still, the merely historical aspect is of little interest here. The point is not so much Plato's stance or, of course, the specific myth of man's primordial fall. The question raised here has a much broader significance; it does not at all center on a philosophical epoch of the past, "great" as it might have been. It concerns the philosopher of our own time and his inner situation.

[2] Plato *Politeia* 474b 5.
[3] Ibid., 475c 3.
[4] Ibid., 486a 5; 485b 5.

This is the question: Is it permissible for the philosopher also to include in his philosophizing reflection information about the world and human existence *not* stemming from experience and rational argumentation but coming from areas such as are properly called "revelation", "sacred tradition", "faith", or "theology"? Can the inclusion of such non-empirical and preter-rational assertions into one's philosophizing possibly be justified? My answer to this: it is not only possible and justified but indeed necessary.

This thesis now requires an immediate defense against certain potential misunderstandings. We have to clarify, above all, what it does *not* imply.

We are not considering—first—philosophy "as such" here; rather, as is the case in the quoted text from Plato's *Politeia,* we consider the existential approach to philosophy and the person of the philosopher. The question here, therefore, is not whether or not a systematic discourse on philosophical problems should also admit theological statements. It may well be that even this question should not be answered with a simple "no". But this is not the topic of our discussion here. The topic is the following contention: suppose a philosopher has personally accepted as true certain preter-rational statements on reality and existence; that is, he does not entertain any doubt about their truth, though not uncritically or naïvely. Suppose further that he explicitly disregards this conviction of his in his philosophical discourse. He would then immediately cease to be an honest philosopher, because from that moment on he would no longer consider his subject matter, the world and existence as such, "under every conceivable aspect".

Such inclusion, incidentally, does not amount to meddling in theology on the part of the philosopher; just as he does not already begin research in physics by considering the results of quantum mechanics in his reflection on the "essence" of matter. The true potential of a philosophical effort is not so much determined, as a rule, by the more or less extensive knowledge of scientific data but rather by the greater or lesser truth of its faith-based premises. Obviously, the decisive question is whether we really have at our disposal such supernatural knowledge and what would make us so certain. This, however, is a question different from the one we are discussing here. The conviction as to the *fact* of what is called *theios logos,* God addressing man, and as to our ability, further, to discern and perceive such revelation—this conviction is not the point of our discussion here; it is explicitly presumed. But let us at least specify to some extent what is meant by some of the terms employed in this context.

"Revelation" denotes the primary and original instance of communication, entirely beyond human comprehension, in which the divine utterance becomes "audible" at all; this was meant by Plato when he spoke prophetically of "an unknown Prometheus bringing down to us the divine message".[5]

"Sacred tradition": this means the act of handing on and receiving from one generation to the next, through which the unique original revelation is kept present in history.[6]

"Faith" is the personal act of assent in which the divine locution, reaching our ear in the way just men-

---

[5] Plato *Philebus* 16c 5ff.

[6] Cf. Josef Pieper, *Über den Begriff der Tradition* (Cologne and Opladen, 1958), 13ff.

tioned, is accepted as true because of its provenience.

"Theology", finally, is the attempt to interpret such supernatural knowledge, in faith accepted as truth, as to its genuine meaning.[7]

Second, there is every indication that man, whenever he searches, philosophizing, into the meaning of the world and his existence as such, inevitably falls back on convictions that are "preter-rational" at least in the sense of being unprovable either through experience or rational argumentation. This is true even in those instances where the individual is not aware of such recourse, or explicitly rejects it. Any philosophy that claims, in this sense, to be "without presuppositions" becomes rather peculiar insofar as its presuppositions, to use T. S. Eliot's remark about "certain philosophers", simply "remain equally unknown to the author as to the reader".[8]

Even where the rejection of any "sacred tradition" is made into a principle—not merely to set it aside methodologically but explicitly to deny and refuse its content—even there such rejection takes on the character of a creed, whether or not one is aware of it and comfortable with it.

It is ever anew amazing to see, for example, how unaware Jean-Paul Sartre seems to be of this situation. It is well known that he expressly understands existentialism as the attempt to pursue in strict reasoning all the consequences resulting from the nonexistence of God.[9] He evidently does not at all realize that he presup-

---

[7] Cf. Josef Pieper, *Hinführung zu Thomas von Aquin,* 2nd ed. (Munich, 1963), 205ff.

[8] T. S. Eliot, Postscript to J. Pieper, *Was heisst Philosophieren?,* 124.

[9] Sartre, *L'Existentialisme,* 94.

poses this nonexistence, uncritically and without the shadow of any justification, much more as a tenet of "faith" than the traditional philosophy ever presupposed the notion of the world as creation. True, he sets out with an explicit interpretation of the traditional concept of "creation"; and nobody can discuss his basic thesis without also discussing this (grotesquely mistaken)[10] interpretation of his. But I suspect that Sartre, while rejecting any assertion about God and creation with the utmost nonchalance, would declare all arguments against such a rejection as "philosophically inadmissible", even though both, arguments and rejection, would logically pertain to the same mental department. Which is not such an unusual sham, after all. Still, Sartre's philosophy, precisely because of the resolute and straightforward identification of its underlying nonnegotiable articles of faith, displays the immediate existential relevance that will always be the distinguishing mark of all serious philosophy. Academic sophistry, in contrast, considers it a matter of discretion to conceal its basic stance, if present at all, and so remains in its core and by necessity irrelevant.

Again, I am convinced that, without exception, every philosophical interpretation of world and human existence relies, at least subconsciously, on certain general assumptions which are not so much "knowledge" as rather "belief". The following reflections will nonetheless consider—*third*—only those situations in which the philosopher is also explicitly a believer who openly accepts the truth of a sacred tradition and consciously tries to be aware of it in his reasoning. Such a believer, in a Western cultural context, will more than likely

[10] Ibid., 19f.

be a Christian. True, Christian doctrine is primarily concerned with offering salvation, not with interpreting reality or human existence. But it implies as well certain fundamental teachings on specifically philosophical matters—the world and existence as such.

Our thesis, to be considered here, states in particular: To claim existential honesty as a Christian philosopher, you cannot disregard the truths of divine revelation that you have accepted in faith.

In the philosophical literature of our time two important voices are raised, each for its own reasons, against this assertion; both, however, are highly representative: the voices of Martin Heidegger and Karl Jaspers.

Heidegger states that anyone who accepts the biblical creation account as truth will always remain "a stranger to the primordial force"[11] of philosophical questioning because he already claims to possess the answer to the question—indeed, the answer to the one question that constitutes philosophy as such:[12] Why is there anything at all and not, rather, nothing? "The very content of our question is folly to the Faith. Philosophy consists in this folly. A 'Christian philosophy' is a wooden iron and a misconception."[13]

Jaspers asserts as well that religious faith and philosophy are incompatible, though—as mentioned—for a different reason: no "honest person can escape the choice between religion and philosophy . . . it means either renouncing independence . . . or renouncing revelation."[14] Faith here is conceived, entirely correctly, as to-

---

[11] Heidegger, *Einführung in die Metaphysik*, 5.
[12] Heidegger, "Das Fragen dieser Frage ist das Philosophieren", ibid., 10.
[13] Ibid., 6.
[14] Jaspers, *Philosophie*, 258.

tal trust in someone whose authority I acknowledge. Precisely this attitude, however, would not be permissible for the philosopher. "Authority is the specific enemy of philosophy"; any reason adduced to justify submission to authority "renounces freedom".[15] All this, I should quickly add, shows only a partial aspect of Jaspers' much more differentiated total conception of the relationship between philosophy and religion. ("Philosophy, in fact, springs from the soil of a religious substance whose explicit manifestation it simultaneously opposes.")[16] Yet the dimension pertinent to our context here is clearly and definitely part of his thinking.

Put in a nutshell, all this reads: A believer cannot also be a philosopher, and vice versa—a philosopher cannot be a believer. On closer examination of the way philosophy is implicitly conceived and defined in these propositions, we discover a somewhat strange fact: both theses emphasize a certain aspect that was hardly relevant, if present at all, in the accepted idea of philosophy from Plato to Kant.

First, however, we return to Heidegger's position, which after all raises some further intriguing questions. Does he not fail to grasp the very essence of faith? Faith, indeed, implies precisely the *absence* of assured knowledge, in spite of all "revelation". This is why the theologian speaks of the "truths of faith" that "nevertheless remain hidden".[17] And regarding "the single" philosophical question: "Why is there anything at all?"— this question, through revelation and faith rather accentuated than silenced, assumes its utmost weight and

[15] Ibid., 265.

[16] Ibid., 269.

[17] M. J. Scheeben, *Die Mysterien des Christentums* (Freiburg im Breisgau, 1941), 8f.

urgency in view of the totally "uncaused" Divine Being. But we cannot pursue this further here. Our interest, rather, centers on the radical challenge of Heidegger's insistence on philosophy as "absolute questioning". "To *endure*—questioning and defenseless—amid the uncertainty of *being* as such", he even claims, would be "the highest form of knowledge".[18]

At this point one might perhaps look up in surprise and reply with the question: Am I myself not saying exactly the same thing? Have I not already explicitly discussed philosophy's intrinsic structure of hope as well as the questioning reflection on reality as such, a questioning that can never be stilled by any final or exhaustive answer? Yes, I have. Any similarity, nonetheless, exists only in appearance. The difference, to put it bluntly and somewhat aggressively, lies in this: for me, "questioning" means to be aware of the elusiveness of any final answer yet nevertheless to pursue such an answer and remain open to it. For Heidegger, in contrast, "questioning" seems to mean the absolute exclusion and rejection of any possible answer (which answer, in fact, would infringe on the purity of questioning itself).

Karl Jaspers' position, too, presents problems in several respects. I ask myself, for instance, what "renouncing revelation" might possibly mean—after all, does "revelation" not mean that God has spoken to man? But we cannot pursue this question, either. We are concerned here with Jaspers' specific conception of philosophy. It seems to be distinguished by its emphasis on the philosopher's independence. The philosopher, of course, is definitely searching for answers, yet not so

[18] M. Heidegger, *Die Selbstbehauptung der deutschen Universität* (Breslau, 1933), 12f.

absolutely as to be willing to accept them from someone else. This emphasis, I believe, is not entirely absent in the traditional conception of philosophy, but it is nearly irrelevant there.

Both positions, Jaspers' as well as Heidegger's, have in common a downright jealous vigilance regarding the purity and integrity of the formal approach to philosophy. The "purity" of the philosophical method seems to be almost more important than the answer to the philosophical question itself. This precisely is the decisive difference from the thinking found in the mainstream of Western philosophy. We may also assert that Plato and Aristotle, in this sense, entirely lacked interest in "philosophy", at least as regards a clearly and formally defined academic discipline, and were not at all concerned with borderlines as such. Instead, their relentlessly probing minds were totally engaged in an attempt to bring into view and define the ultimate nature of human virtue, of Eros, of reality in general. Their inquiry was directed by no other concern than the search for answers to these questions—be those answers ever so vulnerable and fragmentary, and above all: no matter what quarter they came from.

Socrates, in Plato's writings, was never embarrassed to admit that the ultimate, the ontologically decisive truths were known to him not by his own accomplishments but *ex akoēs,* "because he heard them".[19] And the proximity of the rational argument to the mythic tradition, a distinctive feature of nearly all of Plato's

---

[19] Cf. Plato *Phaedo* 61d; *Phaedrus* 235c; *Timaeus* 20d. This expression, which is found *verbatim* also in the Greek of the New Testament ("Faith comes from what is heard"; Rom 10:17), in German translations of Plato is usually rendered as "from hearsay", which obviously is not only incorrect but outright false.

Dialogues, means exactly the same. In Aristotle's much more "scientific" philosophy such a willingness to listen to preter-rational answers is less evident. Yet it has convincingly been shown that "his metaphysics, too, imply the principle of *credo ut intelligam* [I believe in order to understand]".[20] Even Immanuel Kant still stands in this very same tradition, though similarly not in blatant and explicit terms. Thus it comes as quite a surprise to hear him, eight years after *The Critique of Pure Reason,* when he calls the New Testament "an everlasting guide to true wisdom" from which our mind "receives new light in contemplating those things which our mind fails to grasp yet always needs for its instruction".[21]

How, then, would the correlation between knowledge and faith be a concrete part of the philosophical discourse, and how could it be formally and theoretically defined? This is a further and extremely complicated question; still, at least we shall consider it briefly.

We stated so far that the philosopher who is existentially also a believer would have to "respect" the truths of divine revelation, would have to "include" and "consider" them. At the very least he must not "ignore" them nor "isolate" them from his reasoning. These expressions may indeed be helpful approximations. Yet possibly they tend to obscure the infinite difficulty inherent in any attempt to legitimize the connection between the two realms of inquiry. The distinction between knowledge and faith remains essentially unbridged; these are clearly two different things that we try to connect in such a way that each preserves its own form and

[20] Werner Jaeger, *Aristoteles* (Berlin, 1923), 404.
[21] Immanuel Kant, draft of a letter to Heinrich Jung-Stilling, spring 1789, *Briefe von und an Kant,* ed. Ernst Cassirer, vol. 1 (Berlin, 1918), 381.

dignity. There can be no question, therefore, of any homogenous intermingling of the two. On the other hand, though, the notion of a methodically exact delineation of their respective turf, and thus the notion of "border violation", remains quite atypical for the philosopher as well as the theologian, should it appear at all. Neither the one nor the other is entitled to claim every other scientist's obvious prerogative and say, "This is of interest to me, that is not." For both must invariably deal with the "universal, with totality, with things divine and human".[22] Right from the start, then, we must brace ourselves for almost insurmountable difficulties in any attempt to describe adequately the specifics of the connection in question here.

In this we should not despise symbolic images. A truly striking analogy has the advantage of presenting to the inner eye a simple image without destroying the *arcanum* [mystery] that indeed permeates all reality.

To explain the correlation of knowledge and faith, the image of a polyphonic counterpoint immediately makes sense. In such a composition, independent melodies correlate with each other, accentuate, challenge, perhaps even disturb each other in such a way as to create a fresh, rich, and captivating harmony that can no longer be explained by merely adding together its individual components.

It may well be more than merely an "image" to call the believer "a listener". Is there any way to express it more accurately? A believer neither "knows" nor "sees" with his own eyes; he accepts the testimony of someone else. Much of this testimony, indeed, regards the same universe that his own eyes behold, and that

---

[22] Plato *Politeia* 486a 5.

he, as scientist or philosopher, investigates using his own faculties. Such testimony may even guide his attention or sharpen his perception so that he suddenly sees with his own eyes what otherwise would have remained hidden, had he not heeded and pondered the message reaching him from elsewhere. The clarifying power of such an image is evident. It makes quite clear, for example, that Karl Jaspers' inescapable alternative of faith *or* philosophy is entirely nonexistent. Why should I be compelled to choose in favor of "hearing" and against the use of my own eyes, and vice versa? What could prevent me from accepting both: seeing and hearing, philosophy and faith? And then, who could ever determine the pattern and structure according to which knowing and believing also mix and intermingle in the common everyday activity of the human mind?

In fact, nowhere is it written that explicit rules for the correlation of knowledge and faith may be possible at all. Besides, we face here more than just a theoretical difficulty. Such a correlation needs to be lived, and this within the infinitely variable context of a concrete existence. Conflicts here are not only possible but downright inevitable, as the natural concomitants of mental progress. We may even go so far as to recognize the mark of a truly philosophical attitude whenever such conflicts are serenely faced and patiently endured, without the ready inclination toward hasty harmonization or premature capitulation. The statement comes to mind that says that a philosophy truly embracing all attainable information is superior, not because it would be able to offer smoother answers but because it will bring out more clearly the dimension of mystery that pervades all reality.

In the end it may not be overly important to search

for a theoretical formula that would assign with utmost accuracy its specific function to faith, knowledge, and philosophy alike. It is more decisive to live out that unrestrained, all-embracing openness that is not so much an attitude or virtue of the human mind, but rather its very essence, its nature itself.

INDEX

absolute, 14
acceptance, 53, 54
Alamogordo, 93
Alcibiades, 92
aliquid, 61, 67
Anaxagoras, 59
Aquinas, Thomas, 59,
    71; on knowledge, 46,
    61, 89; quoted, 55, 64,
    74, 94; on various
    topics, 53, 58, 62, 73, 98,
    99
argumentation, 60, 111
Aristotle, 51, 55, 59, 64; and
    philosophy, 28, 71, 83,
    116, 117; on seeing, 62,
    63; on various topics, 42–
    43, 46, 53, 66, 89–90, 91,
    98, 99
artistic endeavor, 33–35. *See
    also* fine arts; poetry
attitude, 74, 120. *See also*
    critical attitude
Augustine, Saint, 25, 52, 62,
    75, 98
authority, 92, 114, 118

Bacon, Francis, 47
beatific vision, 62, 63
being, 63, 66, 67, 74, 91, 100;
    as object of philosophy,
    60, 64, 71, 88
bonum commune, 59
bonum hominis, 59
bonum utile, 21
Boveri, Margret, 93–94
Brecht, Berthold, 36
Bremond, Henri, 24
Brentano, Franz, 31

Carnap, Rudolf, 18
catharsis, 25–26, 34, 37
Chenu, M. D., 95
Christianity, 75, 112–13,
    117. *See also* faith; reli-
    gion
clarity, 96, 97, 98, 99, 100,
    101. *See also* language;
    lucidity; precision
cognition, 60, 73–74, 77, 79,
    88, 91
comprehendere, 73. *See also*
    understanding
consciousness, 64

contemplation, 38, 47, 53, 59, 61, 63
controversy, 11–12, 95
counterfeit, 34–38
creation, 112, 113
critical attitude, 51, 88

death, 34, 68, 91, 98, 101; and philosophy, 25, 50, 62
Descartes, René, 30
desire, 54, 55, 63, 108
Dewey, John, 30
dialogue, 12, 80, 95
Dilthey, Wilhelm, 20, 34, 105
Diogenes Laertius, 59
Diotima, 71
discussion, 11–12, 44, 102–3
Divine Being. *See* God
Dudinzew, Wladimir, 29

efficiency, 20, 34, 42
Einstein, Albert, 95
Eliot, T. S., 89, 111
empiricism, 14, 20, 76, 79, 103
Engels, Friedrich, 18, 77
enjoyment, 52–53
ens, 67. *See also* being
entertainment, 36, 39, 63
Eros, 25–26, 34, 37, 108, 116
essence, 19, 71, 72, 107
everyday life, 24–26, 27–28, 36, 65, 99

exact sciences. *See* science
exactness, 13, 87–89, 90, 92, 94. *See also* precision
existence, 48, 54, 75, 79, 94. *See also* human existence
existentialism, 111–12
experience, 14–15, 76, 95, 103–5, 111

faith, 109, 112, 113, 120; definition of, 110–11; and knowledge, 114, 117–18; or philosophy, 113, 114, 119. *See also* religion
Fechner, Gustav, 79
Fichte, Johann, 14–15
fine arts, 33, 36, 37, 89. *See also* artistic endeavor; poetry
forms, 14
freedom, 28, 38, 42, 55, 91, 114; and philosophy, 42, 43–46; and science, 51–52. *See also* indepenence
frui. See enjoyment

God, 33, 35, 37, 62, 79, 94, 115; as Creator, 54, 76; existence of, 111–12; and knowability, 74–75, 78; and man, 58, 68, 110
Goethe, Johann, 36, 38, 50
Good, the, 59
Great Soviet Encyclopedia, 30
Guardini, Romano, 75

Hager, Kurt, 36, 37
Hegel, Georg, 14, 39, 97
Heidegger, Martin, 28, 41, 99, 113–16
Herder, Johann, 38, 50
hope, 86, 94, 115
human existence, 57, 60, 65, 68, 102; and hope, 86, 94. *See also* existence
human nature, 63, 76, 120
human spirit, 64–65. *See also* man
Husserl, Edmund, 31

idea, 98
independence, 44, 45, 46, 113, 115–16, 118. *See also* freedom

Jaeger, Werner, 117
Jaspers, Karl, 19, 83, 113–16, 119
justice, 9, 28

Kant, Immanuel, 71, 104, 114, 117
knowability, 72–74, 76, 78, 79, 81, 96
knowledge, 29–30, 61, 73, 89, 98; and faith, 108, 110, 111, 114, 117–20; and freedom, 43, 46, 55; gaining, 47–48, 103, 104; and philosophy, 17, 71, 72, 86–88, 90, 92; and questioning, 14, 115; and science, 19, 86, 88

language, 95–102, 105; everyday, 16–17, 98, 101; and philosophy, 97; and precision, 13, 96, 100, 102; and science, 97; and translation, 98–99. *See also* clarity
law, 28
Lawrence, Nathaniel, 87
Lenin, Vladimir, 18, 77
liberal arts, 42, 46
listening, 11, 47–48, 118–19. *See also* openness; silence
Logos. *See* God
love, 53, 54, 72. *See also* Eros
lucidity, 74, 79, 81. *See also* clarity
Luther, Martin, 50
Luyten, Norbert, 107

magic, 35–36
man, 15, 59, 107–8; condition of, 65, 86, 108; and God, 110, 115; as maker, 77–78, 93; nature of, 63, 107–8; and philosophy, 12, 60, 86. *See also* human spirit; person
Marxism, 18, 52, 77
meaningfulness, 12, 43, 57–59, 63, 66, 67
mirandum. See wonder
Müller, G. E., 30

nature, 52, 54; and science, 47, 92, 93

123

Newman, J. H., 55
Nietzsche, Friedrich, 54,
    98
Nink, Caspar, 91

object, 15, 38, 72, 73
objectivity, 16, 38, 49, 60
openness, 38, 48–49, 51, 60,
    74, 120. *See also* listening;
    silence
Oppenheimer, Robert J., 94

Parmenides, 91
perception, 16, 17, 18, 47,
    73, 74, 104
person, 57–58. *See also* hu-
    man spirit; man
philosophy, 39, 59, 116; act
    of, 23–25, 28–29, 53, 66,
    79; and authority, 114;
    and clarity, 96–97, 99,
    100, 101; and contem-
    plation, 38, 47, 53, 59,
    63; definition of, 12–21,
    29–30, 46, 55, 60, 64, 90;
    differences between, and
    science, 47, 79–80, 91–
    94; and experience, 14–
    15, 105, 111; and free-
    dom, 42–46; fulfillment
    of, 71, 80, 85; and hope,
    86, 94; and knowability,
    71–74, 79, 80–81, 85; and
    knowledge, 17, 71, 72,
    86–88, 90, 92; and lan-
    guage, 97–102; meaning-
    fulness of, 12, 43, 57–59,

63, 66, 67; methods of,
    11, 14, 23, 116; and po-
    etry, 33–35, 99–100; and
    precision, 98, 100–101,
    102; quest of, 20–21, 24–
    25, 28, 50, 51, 63–64, 72,
    78, 101–2; and reality,
    18, 67, 71, 78, 100, 105,
    116, 119; and religion,
    33–35, 120; and science,
    50–51, 83–90, 95, 97,
    102–3, 105, 107; and to-
    talitarianism, 54–55;
    true, 49, 50, 78; and
    truth, 14, 55, 63–64; and
    usefulness, 31, 41–42, 83;
    various systems of, 14–
    15, 26, 75, 111–12; and
    wisdom, 72, 89, 101–2,
    108; and world, 29–30,
    90, 99–100; and world of
    production, 28–29, 30–
    31, 33. *See also* true phi-
    losopher
Plato, 47, 68, 92, 109; and
    philosophy, 17, 26–27,
    72, 83, 116; on religious
    topics, 60, 71, 108, 110,
    114; and *theoria,* 53, 62;
    on various topics, 25, 26,
    98, 118
poetry, 24, 33, 34–37, 92,
    99–100. *See also* artistic
    endeavor; fine arts
positivism, 18, 105
potentia, 91
practical philosophy, 30, 37

practicality, 30, 52, 69, 83, 99. *See also* usefulness

prayer, 33, 35

precision, 86, 98, 100–101, 102. *See also* clarity; exactness

progress, 92

propaganda, 34–35, 36, 37

Protagoras, 29

pseudo-philosophy, 37–38

Pythagoras, 72

question, 11, 19, 47, 49–50

questioning, 45, 48; and faith, 113, 114–16; and philosophy, 12, 13–14, 28, 69

rationality, rationalism, 50, 60, 71, 75, 81

real, reality, 28, 45, 54, 66, 67–68, 91; and empiricism, 103; and experience, 103–4; and knowability, 74, 76, 79, 81, 96, 118; and language, 97, 102; and listening, 47–48, 49; and man, 60, 64; and philosophy, 18, 67, 71, 78, 100, 105, 116, 119; and science, 84, 86, 93; structure of, 68, 75; and totality, 88; and true philosopher, 51; and truth, 45–47, 77

realism, 18, 49

reason, 47, 77. *See also* theoria

reflection, 16, 50, 53, 57, 61, 66; and definition of philosophy, 12, 13, 20

Reichenbach, Hans, 17, 97

religion, 33–36, 37; and philosophy, 109–120. *See also* Christianity; faith; revelation; sacred tradition; theology

res, 67

res artificiales, 66–67, 77, 78

res naturales, 78

revelation, 109–10, 113, 114, 115, 117. *See also* faith; religion

Rousselot, Pierre, 60

Russell, Bertrand, 87

sacred tradition, 109, 110, 111, 112. *See also* faith; religion

Sartre, Jean-Paul, 67, 76, 77–78, 111–12

Scheler, Professor, Dr. 44

Schelling, Friedrich, 14

Schilpp, P. A., 87

Schlick, M., 86

scholé, 44–45

Scholz, Heinrich, 76

science, sciences, 30, 55, 105; approach of, 18–19, 23, 48–49, 90; and clarity, 97, 100; delineation of, 13, 92–94, 118; exact, 14, 48, 95; and freedom, 51–52; and knowability,

76–77, 78–79; and language, 97–98, 100–101; and philosophy, 47, 50–51, 79–80, 83–90, 92–94, 102, 107; and sin, 94, 108; world view of, 18, 85–86, 95. *See also* empiricism

scientific philosophy, 14, 17–18, 84

seeing, 61–62, 75, 118–19

Seel, Otto, 48

self, 16, 39

silence, 11, 47–49, 101

simplicity, 50, 60

sin, 94, 108

socialism, 36

society, 28, 30, 44, 58

Socrates, 26–28, 92, 98, 116

Sophists, sophistry, 29, 38–39, 112

Stalin, Joseph, 77

subject, 16, 38

success, 35, 62

Szilasi, W., 62

Teilhard de Chardin, Pierre, 61–62

Thales, 26–27

Theodorus, 27

theology, 109–10, 111, 118. *See also* faith; religion

theoria (philosophical reasoning), 43, 54, 62, 63; and contemplation, 53; and listening, 47–48; and man, 59, 60; and philoso-

phy, 43, 55, 64, 73; and science, 50–51; and truth, 45–47

Thracian maidservant, 26–27, 67

totalitarianism, 30, 41, 44, 54–55

totality, 16, 49, 54, 88; and definition of philosophy, 14–15, 18, 19; and human spirit, 64, 65–66; and knowability, 74–75, 76–77; and philosophy, 12, 68, 85, 108, 118, 119; and science, 18, 19, 94, 105, 118

true philosopher, 17, 26–27, 38, 72, 54, 108; and openness, 49–51

truth, 11–12, 21, 52, 59, 74; and freedom, 45, 46; and listening, 47–48; and philosophy, 14, 55, 63–64; and reality, 45–47; and religion, 110–11; and science, 51, 84

ultimate meaning, ultimate reasons, 24, 25, 28, 34, 93, 116; and philosophy, 12, 17, 18, 19, 20, 34

understanding, 18, 73, 79, 97, 101, 110. *See also* knowability; knowledge

use (*uti*), 52, 53

usefulness, 36, 38, 45, 54, 58, 65; and philosophy,

20–21, 31, 35, 41–42, 43, 83. *See also* meaningfulness, practicality
utilitarianism, 27, 35, 51–52

virtue, 116

Whitehead, Alfred North, 12–13, 68, 87–88, 96, 104–5
whole of reality. *See* totality
Wild, John, 38
wisdom, 29, 72, 89, 108, 117
Wittgenstein, Ludwig, 90, 96

wonder (*mirandum*), 17, 65–66, 99, 102
workaday. *See* everyday life
world, 52, 54, 68; as creation, 75, 112; and knowability, 79, 81; and man, 64, 65–66; and perception, 104; and philosophy, 29–30, 90, 99–100; and science, 90, 94; and *theoria,* 45, 48
world of production, 30–31, 33, 54